Guilt and Its Vicissitudes

Guilt and Its Vicissitudes: Psychoanalytic Reflections on Morality focuses on the way Melanie Klein and successive generations of her followers pursued and deepened Freud's project of explaining man's moral sense as a wholly natural phenomenon.

With the introduction of the superego, Freud laid claim to the study of moral development as part of the psychoanalytic enterprise. At the same time he reconceptualized guilt: he thought of it not only as conscious, but as unconscious as well, and it was the unconscious sense of guilt that became a particular concern of the discipline he was founding. As Klein saw it, his work merely pointed the way. Judith M. Hughes argues that Klein and contemporary Kleinians went on to provide a more consistent and comprehensive psychological account of moral development. Hughes shows how Klein and her followers came to appreciate that moral and cognitive questions are complexly interwoven and makes clear how this complexity prompted them to extend the range of their theory.

Hughes demonstrates both a detailed knowledge of the major figures in post-war British psychoanalysis, and a keen sensitivity to the way clinical experience informed theory-building. She writes with vigor and grace not only about Freud and Klein, but also about such key thinkers as Riviere, Isaacs, Heimann, Segal, Bion and Joseph. *Guilt and Its Vicissitudes* speaks to those concerned with the clinical application of psychoanalytic theory and to those interested in the contribution psychoanalysis makes to understanding questions of human morality.

Judith M. Hughes is a professor of history and an adjunct professor of psychiatry at the University of California, San Diego. She has written several books including *From Obstacle to Ally: The Evolution of Psychoanalytic Practice* (Routledge, 2004).

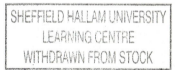

Also by Judith M. Hughes

To the Maginot Line: The Politics of French Military Preparation in the 1920's (1971)

Emotion and High Politics: Personal Relations at the Summit in Late Nineteenth-Century Britain and Germany (1983)

Reshaping the Psychoanalytic Domain: The Work of Melanie Klein, W. R. D. Fairbairn, and D. W. Winnicott (1989)

From Freud's Consulting Room: The Unconscious in a Scientific Age (1994)

Freudian Analysts/Feminist Issues (1999)

From Obstacle to Ally: The Evolution of Psychoanalytic Practice (2004)

Guilt and Its Vicissitudes

Psychoanalytic reflections on morality

Judith M. Hughes

Routledge
Taylor & Francis Group

LONDON AND NEW YORK

First published 2008 by Routledge
27 Church Road, Hove, East Sussex BN3 2FA

Simultaneously published in the USA and Canada
by Routledge
270 Madison Avenue, New York, NY 10016

Routledge is an imprint of the Taylor & Francis Group, an Informa business

© 2008 Judith M. Hughes

Typeset in Times by Garfield Morgan, Swansea, West Glamorgan
Printed and bound in Great Britain by TJ International Ltd, Padstow, Cornwall
Paperback cover design by Lisa Dynan

This publication has been produced with paper manufactured to strict
environmental standards and with pulp derived from sustainable forests.

British Library Cataloguing in Publication Data
A catalogue record for this book is available from the British Library

Library of Congress Cataloging-in-Publication Data
Hughes, Judith M.
   Guilt and its vicissitudes : psychoanalytic reflections on morality / Judith M.
Hughes.
        p. ; cm.
   Includes bibliographical references and index.
   ISBN 978-0-415-43597-0 (hardback) – ISBN 978-0-415-43598-7 (pbk.) 1.
Psychoanalysis. 2. Guilt–Psychological aspects. 3. Moral development. I.
Title.
   [DNLM: 1. Guilt. 2. Moral Development. 3. Psychoanalytic Theory.
WM 460 H893g 2007]
   RC506.H8464 2007
   616.89'17–dc22

                                                            2007013195

ISBN: 978-0-415-43597-0 (hbk)
ISBN: 978-0-415-43598-7 (pbk)

For
David and Melanie
Jesse and Sophia
and
in memory of Stuart

Contents

Acknowledgments

For lively intellectual exchanges before I was ready to put pen to paper I would like to thank members of the University of California Interdisciplinary Psychoanalytic Consortium and candidates at the San Diego Psychoanalytic Institute. With the first group, I presented a sketch of my general approach, with the second, I tried out bits and pieces of the entire argument. For access to the Melanie Klein Archive and for the comfortable working conditions I enjoyed while examining those materials, I am grateful to the staff of the Wellcome Library, London.

Settling down to write a book may seem like a lonely enterprise – and often it is. But one is not really alone. There is an internal audience that is both constant and changing, sometimes encouraging, sometimes not. I would like to thank those who became part of that audience and whose interest I have counted on. Betty Joseph immediately springs to mind. I thanked her in connection with an earlier project and then met with her again in connection with this one. Those conversations were precious – and my pleasure in them comes back to me when I write about her papers. Hanna Segal and John Steiner, also figures in this study, helped me with other books and left me with vivid memories to which I like to return. Elizabeth Bott Spillius reviewed with me at length the present work, cautioning me about possible pitfalls. I have kept her remarks in mind. My indebtedness to the late Richard Wollheim will be easily spotted by those intrigued by the possible confluence of psychoanalysis and moral philosophy. I started a dialogue with him in California, continued it in London, and am still carrying it on.

Other discussions have taken place in San Diego. For years I have talked to Donald L. Kripke and Edward N. Lee about psychoanalytic matters of mutual interest. With Melford E. Spiro I have chewed over knotty problems and have found that saying it aloud is often enough to get me on my way again. Reva P. Greenburg read the second draft of the manuscript with great care, pointing out places where someone might get confused or lost. I have sought to make her concern for the reader my own.

Abbreviations

IJP   *International Journal of Psycho-Analysis*
JAPA   *Journal of the American Psychoanalytic Association*
SE   Sigmund Freud, *The Standard Edition of the Complete Psycho-logical Works of Sigmund Freud.* Translated from the German under the general editorship of James Strachey (London: Hogarth Press, 1953–1974)

Introduction

"Psycho-analysis," Freud wrote in *The Ego and the Id* (1923), "has been reproached time after time with ignoring the higher, moral, supra-personal side of human nature." He considered the reproach unwarranted.

> [T]here has been a general refusal to recognize that psycho-analytic research could not . . . produce a complete and ready-made theoretical structure, but had to find its way step by step along the path towards understanding the intricacies of the mind. . . . So long as we had to concern ourselves with the study of what is repressed in mental life, there was no need for us to share in any agitated apprehension as to the whereabouts of the higher side of man. But now that we have embarked upon the analysis of the ego we can give an answer to all those whose moral sense has been shocked and who have complained that there must surely be a higher nature in man: "Very true," we can say, "and here we have that higher nature, in . . . [the] super-ego, the representative of our relations to our parents. When we were little children we knew these higher natures, we admired and feared them; and later we took them into ourselves."[1]

With the introduction of the superego, Freud made clear that he regarded the study of moral development as central to psychoanalytic theory. He also made clear how he understood the start of that development. Briefly the account of the superego – something he had worked out over the years – went like this. Its function – prohibition and bearer of standards – could be traced back to censorship, which played a crucial role in *The Interpretation of Dreams* (1900), to shame, disgust, and morality, which turned up repeatedly in *The Three Essays on the Theory of Sexuality* (1905), and to the ego-ideal, which loomed large in "On Narcissism: An Introduction" (1914). Its formation harked back to "Mourning and Melancholia" (1917). There Freud argued that the melancholic identified with an abandoned love object. In identifying with the lost object, the melancholic incorporated or introjected it: he took it into himself, more specifically, he felt he had

devoured it. Then, in *The Ego and the Id*, Freud claimed that the establishment of the critical agency itself – the superego – could be explained along
similar lines. At the same time he spelled out the relations between the
superego and the parents and other authority figures in the child's environment. The superego derived from these figures; it was the incorporated or
introjected version of them. And in Freud's view that incorporation took
place on a massive scale at a particular moment – with the dissolution of
the Oedipus complex. Hence on numerous occasions he referred to the
superego and "the heir to the Oedipus complex."[2] (Note: in this narrative
the "weaker sex" ended up with the weaker superego.)

With the superego in place, guilt acquired a fresh significance – "the
expression of a condemnation of the ego by its critical agency."[3] But
Freud's concern with guilt hardly ranked as new – and his earlier thinking
on the subject figured as part of his legacy. Melanie Klein and her followers
took advantage of this conceptual richness; they exploited and elaborated
Freud's pre-1923 as well as post-1923 theorizing. Perhaps not in a tidy
fashion: the tidiness may be mine, not theirs. I am keen on piecing together
– and giving order to – Kleinian reflections on guilt, its pervasiveness and
superabundance and its simultaneous absence from consciousness. To my
mind, this body of psychoanalytic theory captures most vividly and
poignantly the vicissitudes of man's moral sentiments.

*   *   *

My study starts with a chapter devoted to *Totem and Taboo* and to Freud's
novel approach to ethical concerns by way of the psychoneuroses. By the
chapter's end, three items crucial to the book's organization will have been
introduced. First, ambivalence: drawing freely on his experience with
obsessional neurotics, Freud came to regard ambivalence – the hallmark of
that disorder – as the source of conscience as well. Second, omnipotence of
thought: again based on his clinical work Freud came to appreciate how
people confused the thought with the deed or rather regarded the thought
as sufficient to produce the deed. Third, the prevalence of guilt: a decade
before he conceptualized the superego, Freud was already suggesting that
guilt was virtually inescapable.

The next two chapters take up the two sides of ambivalence. As I see it,
intense love and equally intense hate offer complementary perspectives on
guilt. In Chapter 2 I begin with *Group Psychology and the Analysis of the
Ego*, a text which features the love between followers and leader; from there
I move to Klein's emphasis on the love one feels for a good internal object
and the overwhelming guilt that accompanies damage to it. Could this guilt,
Klein was led to ask, be alleviated? Hence the chapter ends with a consideration of reparation – and how it frequently comes to nought. In
Chapter 3 the superego finally takes center stage. Here I concentrate on the
rendering Freud gave it in *Civilization and Its Discontents*. His effort to

account for its severity – for the hate at its core – borrowed from Klein's writings. In turn she and her followers focused on the feelings of persecution it aroused and the complicated defensive organizations aimed at keeping those feelings in check. Both Chapters 2 and 3 close with guilt essentially unchanged. Both also end with omnipotence of thought figuring as crucial to a person's defending against, warding off, in short, evading unbearable guilt. Questions of moral and cognitive development were obviously mixed up with one another.

In Chapter 4 I take up Klein and her adherents' discussions of an infant's appreciation of reality and how it unfolds. In the 1920s, in connection with disturbances in learning, Klein explored the challenge fantasy posed to that unfolding. Over the next two decades her interest in fantasy waxed; her interest in what, following Freud, she referred to as the epistemophilic instinct waned. Then in the late 1950s, Wilfred R. Bion reintroduced the "impulse of curiosity on which all learning depends" and granted it a status equivalent to that of love and hate.[4] Bion's contribution paved the way for considering how a person's growing ability to face reality – understood as internal or psychic as well as external or material – made possible his becoming not only more reasonable but also more appropriately responsible, how it made possible his emancipation from a punitive superego and his reclaiming a right to pass judgment on himself.

*   *   *

I have said that I am surveying Kleinian thought, and the subtitle of the book – *Psychoanalytic Reflections on Morality* – speaks to my regard for its centrality. Yet there were those, and still may be some (among an older generation) who insisted that Klein and her colleagues did not deserve the appellation psychoanalyst. As late as the mid-1990s, Roy Schafer, an analyst of international repute, writing appreciatively of contemporary Kleinians (for an American psychoanalytic journal) felt called on to address the matter. He did so by referring to his subjects as "Kleinian Freudians." "It is," he explained, "because I see the Kleinian work in the way the Kleinians themselves see it, that is, as a development out of the heart of Freud's thinking."[5]

This was precisely the position Klein and her supporters defended in the Controversial Discussions of the 1940s. What happened was the following. In 1938, shortly after the Nazi annexation of Austria, the Freuds arrived in London, thanks to Ernest Jones's strenuous efforts to procure them British entry and work permits. A little over a year later Freud was dead. Jones strove equally hard to get émigré analysts accepted into the British Psycho-Analytical Society. As Anna Freud subsequently remarked: to persuade the British "to open their doors to the influx of members from Vienna, i.e., to colleagues who held different scientific views from their own and [who] could only be expected to disrupt peace and internal unity" was no mean achievement.[6] In short order "war" broke out: Anna declared that her own work and that of her collaborators was "Freudian analysis . . . and Mrs. Klein's work" was "not psycho-analysis but a substitution for it."[7] Intent on disputing Anna's right to represent "her father's views," Klein urged her followers "to refresh our memory on every word Freud has written. . . . Then we might" confront "the 'Viennese Freudians' on their own ground."[8] In July 1942 the Society decided to devote one scientific meeting a month to an examination of theoretical disagreements. The following October the format of those meetings was determined. It fell to the Kleinians to give the opening papers, and that task devolved on Susan Isaacs and Paula Heimann, as well as on Klein herself. All three took pains, Joan Riviere commented, to show "that many of the concepts . . . developed by . . . Klein were already inherent in the earliest psycho-analytical theory and observations, and that her work" progressed "by natural and logical steps from that." With "each side appearing to claim to be more Freudian than the other," she added, the effect was sometimes "farcical."[9] Not surprisingly, the attempt to reconcile the contending parties failed.

The Kleinians survived the onslaught, both intellectually and institutionally – their papers will crop up in later chapters – despite the fact that the central issue, faithfulness to the master's ideas, was wrongly posed. Isaacs, for one, publicly objected to the implicit injunction "that Freud's work and his conclusions" were "never to be developed any further and that no one" was "to formulate theories which he himself had not yet formed."[10] Klein herself firmly believed that she was "entitled to continue" Freud's findings – a belief that she did not voice very often or very loudly.[11] Of course, she was correct. More to the point, she pursued a project that Freud had barely begun – the project of exploring "the higher, moral . . . side of human nature."

*   *   *

There are two very broad ways of thinking about morality. The first sees it as a set of thoughts or propositions which may be formulated with a high degree of precision or completeness. The second sees it as primarily part of a person's psychology. If one accepts the second view, then moral philosophy is pursued as moral psychology. Both Freud and Klein implicitly took this line. A moral sense, they presumed, is natural but not native: it does not start at birth; it is an emergent phenomenon.[12] So they interested themselves in its history, with Klein and contemporary Kleinians offering the more consistently psychological account. And the more comprehensive: as they came to appreciate the complex interweaving of moral and cognitive questions, they extended the range of their theory. Here judgment as well as conscience found a home.

Chapter 1

An unconscious sense of guilt

When *Totem and Taboo* appeared in 1912–1913, Freud's loyal followers greeted it with unreserved enthusiasm. Even before he had seen it in print, Ernest Jones ventured the opinion that it and "not the *Traumdeutung* [*The Interpretation of Dreams*] would be Freud's 'masterpiece.'"[1] Having had a chance to look at it, Sándor Ferenczi came to the conclusion that it "will one day be the nodal point of the study . . . of civilization."[2] The development of anthropology suggests that Ferenczi's prediction was wildly inaccurate. According to George Stocking, *Totem and Taboo*, with its "bit of highly conjectural history, . . . perhaps more than anything else in Freud, contributed to the alienation of anthropologists from psychoanalytic theory."[3] In one respect, however, analysts and anthropologists were in agreement: they regarded *Totem and Taboo* as a work of applied psychoanalysis, that is, bringing psychoanalysis to bear on ethnographic problems and in the process promising both solutions to those problems and something akin to experimental proof of Freudian postulates.

Totem and Taboo, while marking Freud's first interdisciplinary effort, also signaled a major departure in his thinking about morality. I plan to set aside the anthropological theorizing and to concentrate instead on Freud's ethical concerns, paying close attention to themes that Melanie Klein and her students chose to elaborate.

Freud had earlier written about one aspect of morality – the sexual. His paper "'Civilized' Sexuality Morality and Modern Nervous Illness" (1908), published four years before his essay on taboo, was an unsparing dissection of contemporary sexual ethics. Western society, he argued, with its insistence that both sexes practice abstinence until they married and that all those who remained unwed abstain throughout their lives, was demanding more than the flesh could bear. Marriage itself could not fully compensate for the prior restrictions – in part because even in marriage couples were obliged to content themselves "with a very few procreative acts." Fear of pregnancy, at a time when "all the devices . . . for preventing conception" impaired "sexual enjoyment" or "hurt the finer susceptibilities of both partners," first brought "the married couple's physical affection to an end," and then, as a consequence, usually put a stop "to the mental sympathy between them." Both partners thus found themselves back in the state they had been before their marriage, "except for being the poorer by the loss of an illusion."[4] Once more they found themselves tried to the utmost and at grave risk of nervous illness.

What kind of nervous illness? Here Freud distinguished between "two groups of nervous disorder," the neuroses proper – otherwise known as the actual neuroses – and the psychoneuroses. In both an impaired sexual life figured as the pathogen. In the actual neuroses, the symptoms appeared to be of a "*toxic* nature": they behaved "exactly like the phenomena accompanying an excess or a deprivation of certain nerve poisons." In fact the form taken by the disease corresponded "to the nature of the noxae, so that often enough the particular sexual aetiology" could be "at once deduced from the clinical picture." With the psychoneuroses, the causation was less transparent. Psychoanalysis, however, had made it possible "to recognize that the symptoms of these disorders (hysteria, obsessional neurosis, etc.)" were "*psychogenic*" and depended upon "the operation of unconscious (repressed) ideational complexes." The complexes themselves had a sexual content: they sprang from unsatisfied sexual needs and represented a "substitute satisfaction."[5] By the time Freud sat down to write about "some points of agreement between the mental life of savages and neurotics," he had lost interest in the actual neuroses. By then he had also refashioned his etiological account of the psychoneuroses: he had, after more than a decade of effort, replaced the seduction hypothesis with Oedipus, "the nuclear complex of every neurosis."[6]

Along with this exclusive focus on the psychoneuroses and their oedipal origins, Freud shone a bright light on guilt. What did this entail? To explore morality by way of the psychoneuroses meant, in the first instance, never forgetting the neurotic's frequent "disregard of reality testing."[7] It meant, in the second instance discriminating among the psychoneuroses to find the best guide or guides. Freud turned explicitly to obsessional neurosis and phobia. (Hysteria showed up too, but its appearance was unheralded.) By the time he had completed *Totem and Taboo* – a decade before he formulated his notion of a superego – Freud was ready to suggest that guilt was well nigh inevitable.

The omnipotence of thoughts

> Neurotics live in a world apart, where . . . only "neurotic currency" is legal tender; that is to say, they are only affected by what is thought with intensity and pictured with emotion, whereas agreement with external reality is a matter of no importance.[8]

For this "overvaluation of mental processes," Freud used the term "omnipotence of thoughts."[9] He had taken it from a highly intelligent obsessional neurotic: Ernst Lanzer, a.k.a. the Rat Man. On October 1, 1907, the 29-year old, university-educated, man had shown up in Freud's consulting room. Ever since childhood he had been harassed by persistent worries. He mentioned, as an example, a compulsion to cut his throat with a straight razor. Just when "he was in the middle of a very hard piece of work the idea had occurred to him: 'If you received a command to take your examination this term at the first possible opportunity, you might manage to obey it. But if you were commanded to cut your throat . . ., what then?' He had at once become aware that this command had already been given, and was hurrying to the cupboard to fetch his razor."[10] Years of his life, he complained on first meeting Freud, had been wasted fighting such compulsions, commands, and prohibitions.

Ernst believed that his thoughts and feelings and wishes, whether good or bad, were omnipotent. He cited the following instance:

> When he returned for a second visit to the hydropathic establishment at which his disorder had been relieved for the first and only time, he asked to be given his old room, for its position had facilitated his relations with one of the nurses. He was told that the room was already taken and that it was occupied by an old professor. This piece of news considerably diminished his prospects of successful treatment, and he reacted to it with the unamiable thought: "I wish he may be dead for it!" A fortnight later he was woken from his sleep by the disturbing idea of a corpse; and in the morning he heard that the professor had really had a stroke, and that he had been carried up to his room at about the time he himself had woken up.[11]

Neurotics – and not just obsessional neurotics – might live in this world of omnipotent thoughts. But they were not its only inhabitants. Children also resided there. By the time Ernst came for treatment, the equation neurotic equals infantile was an already well-established feature of Freud's thought.

*   *   *

In his paper "Formulations on the Two Principles of Mental Functioning" (1911), Freud distinguished between the pleasure and reality principles and postulated how the latter came to replace the former.

> [T]he state of psychical rest was originally disturbed by the peremptory demands of internal needs. When this happened, whatever was thought of (wished for) was simply presented in a hallucinatory manner, just as still happens with our dream-thoughts every night. It was only the non-occurrence of the expected satisfaction, the disappointment experienced, that led to the abandonment of this attempt at satisfaction by means of hallucination. Instead of it, the psychical apparatus had to

decide to form a conception of the real circumstances in the external world and to endeavour to make a real alteration in them. A new principle of mental functioning was thus introduced; what was presented in the mind was no longer what was agreeable but what was real. . . . This setting up of the *reality principle* proved a momentous step.[12]

A step, however, that was never taken once and for all: "With the introduction of the reality principle one species of thought activity was split off; it was kept free from reality-testing and remained subordinated to the pleasure principle alone. This activity is *phantasying*, which begins already in children's play, and later, continued as *day-dreaming*, abandons dependence on real objects."[13]

It was along this dimension, that is, of the relation to reality, that Freud discerned a similarity not only between neurotics and children but between children and "primitives." Neurotics, children, and primitives all inhabited the realm of omnipotent thoughts.

*　　*　　*

Primitive peoples (and not just primitive peoples), Freud wrote, are convinced "that human individuals are inhabited . . . by spirits," that is, by "souls which live in human beings [,] can leave their habitation and migrate into other human beings"; and are thus "independent of . . . bodies." Beyond that, they populate the whole world – animate and inanimate alike – "with innumerable spiritual beings both benevolent and malignant."[14] How could one protect oneself from the malign? How might one acquire the power to harm one's enemies? These are the questions that magic is supposed to answer.

Freud drew on James G. Frazer to give instances of magic in action. One, for example, consisted in making an effigy of an enemy. Whatever was done to the effigy, the same thing happened "to the detested original": whatever part of the effigy's body was damaged, the same part of the enemy's became diseased. And whether the effigy actually resembled the person it represented – in the Egyptian ritual Freud quoted, it did not – was of little moment.

> Every night when the sun-god Ra sank down to his home in the glowing west he was assailed by hosts of demons under the leadership of he arch-fiend Apepi. . . . To aid the sun-god in this daily struggle, a ceremony was daily performed in his temple at Thebes. A figure of his foe Apepi, represented as a crocodile with a hideous face or a serpent with many coils, was made of wax, and on it the demon's name was written in green ink, the figure was then tied up with black hair, spat upon, hacked with a stone knife, and cast on the ground. There the

priest trod on it with his left foot again and again, and then burnt it in a fire made of a certain plant or grass. . . . The service, accompanied by the recitation of . . . prescribed spells, was repeated not merely morning noon and night, but whenever a storm was raging, or heavy rain set in, or black clouds were stealing across the sky to hide the bright sun's disc. The fiends of darkness, clouds, and rain felt the injuries inflicted on their images as if they had been done to themselves; they passed away at least for a time, and the beneficent sun-god shone out triumphant once more."[15]

This example, and others as well, suggested to Freud that the "explanation of all the folly of magical observances" is the mistaking of an association in thought for a similar connection in reality. Frazer, Freud noted, had earlier reached an identical conclusion: "Man mistook the order of their ideas for the order of nature, and hence imagined that the control which they have, or seem to have, over their thoughts permitted them to exercise a corresponding control over things." At this point Freud expressed some dissatisfaction: "the associative theory of magic merely explains the paths along which magic proceeds; it does not explain its true essence, namely, the misunderstanding which leads it to replace the laws of nature by psychological ones." Some "dynamic factor" was "evidently missing." Here Freud brought omnipotence of thoughts into the discussion: "All we need to suppose is that primitive man had an immense belief in the power of his wishes. The basic reason why what he sets about by magical means comes to pass is, after all, simply that he wills it."[16]

But Freud did not underline what was at stake: thoughts can kill. And given the lessons Ernst Lanzer had already taught him, Freud might have added that primitives are not alone in holding this conviction.

Obsessional neurosis and taboo

"Taboo," wrote Freud, "is a Polynesian word," not easily translated, nor readily defined. One set of meanings suggested the sacred and consecrated; another pointed to the dangerous and forbidden. The two sets had in common "a sense of something unapproachable" that expressed itself in prohibitions and restrictions. Among primitive peoples, the prohibitions were legion: "Every sort of thing is forbidden; but they have no idea why, and it does not occur to them to raise the question. On the contrary they submit to prohibitions as though they were a matter of course and feel convinced that any violation of them will be automatically met by the direst punishment." And it occurred to Freud, and he assumed that it would to his readers as well, "that the moral and conventional prohibitions by which we ourselves are governed may have some essential relationship with . . . primitive taboos."[17]

The forbidden sort of thing that Freud held up as an object-lesson was the restriction on "a man's intercourse with his mother-in-law." This avoidance, he claimed, was more widespread and more strictly enforced than any other. He quoted the following example:

> Among the Eastern Bantu "custom requires that a man should be 'ashamed of' his wife's mother, that is to say, he must studiously shun her society. He may not enter the same hut with her, and if by chance they meet on a path, one or the other turns aside, she perhaps hiding behind a bush while he screens his face with a shield. If they cannot thus avoid each other, and the mother-in-law has nothing else to cover herself with, she will tie a wisp of grass round her head as a token of ceremonial avoidance. All correspondence between the two has to be carried on either through a third party or by shouting to each other at a distance with some barrier, such as a kraal fence, interposed between them. They may not even pronounce each other's proper name."

The restriction might be widespread and strict; but it also seemed excessive. Why, anthropologists wondered, should so many different peoples "feel such great fear of the temptation presented to a man by an elderly woman." Even in "civilized" communities, the mother-in law and son-in-law relation, though no longer subject to explicit prohibition, is "one of the delicate points of family organization. . . . There is scarcely room for doubt that something in the . . . relation . . . makes it hard for them to live together."

> On the side of the mother-in-law there is reluctance to give up the possession of her daughter, distrust of the stranger to whom she is to be handed over, an impulse to retain the dominating position which she has occupied in her own house. On the man's side there is a determination not to submit any longer to someone else's will, jealousy of anyone who possessed his wife's affection before he did, and, last but not least, an unwillingness to allow anything to interfere with the illusory overvaluation bred of his sexual feelings.[18]

All this, Freud implied, was common knowledge. He had something novel to add: the relation between mother-in-law and son-in-law was not simply one of hostility; it was in fact "composed of conflicting affectionate and hostile impulses." Freud set out to locate the affection. As for the mother-in-law:

> A woman whose psychosexual needs should find satisfaction in her marriage and her family life is often threatened with the danger of being left unsatisfied, because her marriage relation has come to a

premature end and because of the uneventfulness of her emotional life. A mother, as she grows older, saves herself from this by putting herself in her children's place, by identifying herself with them; and this she does by making their emotional experiences her own. . . . A mother's sympathetic identification with her daughter can easily go so far that she herself falls in love with the man her daughter loves. . . . And very often the unkind, sadistic components of her love are directed on to her son-in-law in order that the forbidden, affectionate one may be the more severely suppressed.

In a man's relation to his wife's mother, Freud found loving elements as well:

It is regularly found that he chose his mother as the object of his love, and perhaps his sister as well, before passing on to his final choice. . . . The place of his own and his sister's mother is taken by his mother-in-law. He has an impulse to fall back upon his original choice, though everything in him fights against it. . . . A streak of irritability and malevolence that is apt to be present in the medley of his feelings leads us to suspect that she [the mother-in-law] does in fact offer him a temptation to incest; and this is confirmed by the not uncommon event of a man openly falling in love with the woman who is later to be his mother-in-law before transferring his love to her daughter.[19]

At one and the same time Freud made restrictions on contact between son-in-law and mother-in-law understandable – they could now be counted as an instance of the taboo against incest – and unearthed the infantile roots of that taboo. "Psycho-analysis has taught us," he claimed, "that a boy's earliest choice of objects for his love is incestuous and that those objects are forbidden ones – his mother and his sister. . . . [A]s he grows up, he liberates himself from this . . . attraction." It becomes unconscious. With "savage peoples," incestuous wishes are not routinely repressed, and so "they are still regarded . . . as immediate perils against which the most severe measures of defence must be enforced."[20]

*   *   *

"A neurotic," Freud argued, "invariably exhibits some degree of psychical infantilism. He has either failed to get free from the psychosexual conditions that prevailed in his childhood or he has returned to them."[21] It stood to reason, then, that in his work with Ernst Lanzer, Freud would try to locate in his patient's childhood the ambivalence – the "*chronic* co-existence of love and hatred, both directed towards the same person and both of the highest degree of intensity"[22] – that lay at the heart of obsessional neurosis.

At the start of the treatment, Ernst recounted, in a disjointed fashion, what had prompted him to seek Freud's help. A couple of months earlier, while doing his stint as an Austrian reserve officer, he had lost his pince-nez and had wired his optician in Vienna for a replacement. Having sent the telegram, he fell into conversation with a Czech captain, who told him of a terrible punishment practiced in the East. At this point Ernst "broke off, got up from the sofa," and begged Freud "to spare him the recital of the details." Freud refused; he could not grant a request that violated the fundamental injunction of psychoanalysis: say it aloud.

> I went on to say that I would do all I could . . . to guess the full meaning of any hints he gave me. Was he perhaps thinking of impalement? – "No, not that, . . . the criminal was tied up . . ." – he expressed himself so indistinctly that I could not immediately guess in what position – ". . . a pot was turned upside down on his buttocks . . . some *rats* were put into it . . . and they . . ." he had again got up and was showing every sign of horror . . . – ". . . *bored their way in . . .*" – "Into his anus," I helped him out. . . . He proceeded with the greatest difficulty: "At that moment the idea flashed through my mind *that this was happening* to *a person who was very dear to me.*"[23]

The rat punishment, so it had dawned on him, would be visited not only upon a lady he loved very much, but on his father as well. (Here Freud noted dryly that "as his father had died many years previously," fear for him was even "more nonsensical" than fear for his lady.)[24] That evening when the Czech captain had handed Ernst his pince-nez, which in the meantime had arrived, and had told him to reimburse Lieutenant David, a "sanction" had taken shape in his mind: "do not repay the money lest the fantasy become real." Then, in a manner he found familiar, a counter-command had come to him: "you must return" the sum in question to Lieutenant David.[25] He had spent the rest of the day and the next trying to obey the second command. (An official at the post office, he soon discovered, not the lieutenant, had advanced the money for the pince-nez; nonetheless he had remained steadfast in his determination to put the small sum in David's hands.) And he spent the rest of that session and the next trying to narrate his tortured and tortuous efforts to repay the wrong person.

Both Ernst and Freud approached their work together with quite definite expectations. Ernst knew something about Freud's theories, enough to assume that his analyst would inquire about his sexual life, and very early on he proceeded, without any prompting, to tell Freud that that life had been "stunted": masturbation played "a small part in it"; as for intercourse, he had first experienced it at the age of 26, and thereafter "only at irregular intervals." The following day, he returned to this subject – "without any apparent transition":

"I can remember a scene during my fourth or fifth year. . . . We had a very pretty young governess. . . . One evening she was lying on the sofa lightly dressed, and reading. I was lying beside her, and begged her to let me creep under her skirt. She told me that I might, so long as I said nothing to any one about it. She had very little on, and I fingered her genitals and the lower part of her body, which struck me as very queer. After this I was left with a burning and tormenting curiosity to see the female body. . . .

There were certain people, girls, who pleased me very much, and I had a very strong wish *to see them naked*. But in wishing this I had an *uncanny feeling, as though something might happen if I thought such things, and as though I must do all sorts of things to prevent it*."

(In reply to a question, he gave an example of these fears: "For instance, *that my father might die*.")

A few days later Ernst returned to the theme of his sexual life and recounted, with some urgency, an event of his youth:

When he was twelve years old he had been in love with a little girl, the sister of a friend. . . . But she had not shown him as much affection as he had desired. And thereupon the idea had come to him that she would be kind to him if some misfortune were to befall him; and as an instance of such a misfortune his father's death had forced itself upon his mind. . . . He then proceeded to tell me that a precisely similar thought had flashed through his mind a second time, six months before his father's death. At that time he had already been in love with his lady, but financial obstacles made it impossible to think of an alliance with her. The idea had then occurred to him that *his father's death might make him rich enough to marry her*. . . . The same idea, though in a much milder form had come to him for a third time, on the day before his father's death. He had then thought: "Now I may be going to lose what I love most"; and then came the contradiction: "No, there is someone else whose loss would be even more painful to you." These thoughts surprised him very much, for he was quite certain that his father's death could never have been an object of his desire but only of his fear.[26]

At this point Freud began to give some hint of his own quite definite expectations. He had taken for granted that he would find hostility toward the father and was convinced, as he told Ernst, that behind fear of his father's dying lay a death-wish that had been energetically repudiated; and indeed the very intensity of Ernst's love for his father signaled a repressed (and equally intense) hatred. Freud also assumed that the hatred had something to do with "*sensual desires*."[27] "Hatred for the father as strong as in this case" could "arise only if the father" had "disturbed the child in his sexuality."[28] Before long Freud found an opportunity to offer his patient a "construction" of what had happened. Ernst had told of "curiosity" about masturbation coming "over him in his twenty-first year, *shortly after his father's death*." He had told of the shame he had felt "each time he gave way to this kind of gratification" and of the vow he had made to forswear such activities. It had been a self-imposed prohibition that he had not abided by. He had told of the occasions on which he had violated it, and Freud "could not help pointing out that these . . . occasions had something in common – a prohibition, and the defiance of a command." Prompted by this material Freud suggested that when Ernst "was a child under six" he had been "soundly castigated by his father" for masturbation; that masturbation had come to an end, but the punishment "had left behind . . . an ineradicable grudge against his father and had established him for all time in his role as an interferer with the patient's sexual enjoyment."[29]

Ernst responded to this construction by reporting a childhood scene which he himself did not recall, but which had been repeatedly described to him by his mother. "The tale was as follows."

> When he was very small . . . he had done something naughty, for which his father had given him a beating. The little boy had flown into a terrible rage and had hurled abuse at his father even while he was under his blows. But as he had no bad language, he had called him by all the names of common objects that he could think of, and had screamed: "You lamp! You towel! You plate!" and so on. His father, shaken by such an outburst of elemental fury, had stopped beating him, and had declared: "The child will be either a great man or a great criminal!" . . . His father, he said, never beat him again; and he also attributed to this experience . . . the change which came over his character. From that time forward he was a coward – out of fear of the violence of his own rage.[30]

When Ernst checked with his mother, she confirmed the story, but added that he had been punished for biting someone, not for masturbating. The mother's testimony alone, Freud argued in a long footnote, was not reason enough for him to abandon his insistence on the sexual.

The hostility toward the father – the love was taken for granted – Freud insisted on tracing back to childhood; the hostility toward the lady Ernst loved Freud stamped with a current date. (Only in the long footnote defending his claims about childhood sexuality did he refer to Ernst's "desires for his mother." In the text itself he neglected entirely the connection between mother and lady.")[31] With love and hate now mapped out, Freud was ready to explore the "agreement" between obsessional neurosis and taboo.

*   *   *

Freud presented a number of specimens for consideration – each serving to suggest ambivalence, particularly its hostile aspect, at work in the "observances of taboo."[32]

A prime example – the taboo on rulers – was rife with contradiction. On the one hand kings and the like were privileged and enjoyed what common people were denied; on the other they were restricted by taboos from which ordinary folk were exempt. No ruler labored under more constraints than the Mikado of Japan:

> An account written more than two hundred years ago reports that the Mikado "thinks it would be very prejudicial to his dignity and holiness to touch the ground with his feet; for this reason, when he intends to go anywhere, he must be carried thither on men's shoulders. Much less will they suffer that he should expose his sacred person to the open air, and the sun is not thought worthy to shine on his head. There is such a holiness ascribed to all parts of his body that he dares to cut off neither his hair, nor his beard, nor his nails. . . . [L]est he should grow too dirty, they may clean him in the night when he is asleep. . . . In ancient times he was obliged to sit on the throne for some hours every morning, with the imperial crown on his head, but to sit altogether like a statue, without stirring either hands or feet, head or eyes, nor indeed any part of his body, because, by this means it was thought that he could preserve peace and tranquillity in his empire."

How to account for the fact that the taboo picked out the ruler and exalted him above all other mortals and also made "his existence a torment and intolerable burden" and reduced him "to a bondage far worse than that of his subjects"?[33] Here Freud discerned the effect of ambivalent impulses: in these ceremonies, alongside the conscious love and reverence, unconscious hostility came into play.

A second example – the taboo upon the dead – permitted Freud to expand on the fate that befell or was inflicted upon the hostile component of ambivalence. As his point of departure he took the prohibitions against uttering the name of the deceased.

> [I]n some South American tribes it is regarded as a deadly insult to the survivors to mention the name of the dead relative in their presence, and the punishment for it is not less than that laid down for murder. . . . [T]he Masai in East Africa resort to the device of changing the dead man's name immediately after his death; he may then be mentioned freely under his new name while all the restrictions remain attached to the old one. . . . The Adelaide and Encounter Bay tribes of South

> Australia are so consistently careful that after the death everyone
> bearing the same name as the dead man's, or a very similar one, changes
> it for another. . . . [A]mong certain tribes in Victoria and North-West
> America, this is carried a step further, and after a death all the dead
> person's relations change their names, irrespective of any similarity in
> their sound.

The "mourning savages," Freud continued, were of the opinion that to say
the name of the dead person was tantamount to invoking him and would be
quickly followed by the return of his ghost – and not a friendly ghost at
that. It would seem, so Freud inferred, that at the moment of death a dearly
loved relative changed "into a demon from whom his survivors" could
"expect nothing but hostility and against whose evil desires they must
protect themselves by every possible means." At that very moment the
survivors handed over to the deceased – projected onto was Freud's
technical term – the hostility that had been theirs.

> A hostile current of feeling . . . against a person's nearest and dearest
> relatives may remain latent . . ., that is, its existence may not be
> betrayed to consciousness either directly or through some substitute. . . .
> [W]hen they die, . . . the conflict becomes acute. The mourning which
> derives from an intensification of the affectionate feelings becomes on
> the one hand more impatient of the latent hostility, and, on the other
> hand, will not allow it to give rise to any sense of satisfaction. Accord-
> ingly, there follow the repression of the unconscious hostility by the
> method of projection and the construction of . . . [a] ceremonial which
> gives expression to the fear of being punished by the demons. When . . .
> the mourning runs its course, the conflict grows less acute, so that the
> taboo upon the dead is able to diminish in severity and sink into
> oblivion.[34]

Up to this point the lessons Freud had learned from obsessional neurotics had stood him in good stead. He had begun by outlining the two basic
laws of totemism. The first, the taboo on incest, had led to an extensive
consideration of taboo. Here Freud paused. Before tackling the second, the
law against destroying the totem animal, he found it necessary to return, so
to speak, to the consulting room.

Phobia, hysteria, and totemism

What is totemism? It "is a system which takes the place of a religion among
certain primitive peoples of Australia, America and Africa, and provides
the basis of their social organization." As for its "essential characteristics,"
they are the following: "*Originally, all totems were animals, and were*

regarded as the ancestors of the different clans. Totems were inherited only through the female line. There was a prohibition against killing the totem (or – which under primitive conditions, is the same thing – against eating it). *Members of a totem clan were forbidden to practice sexual intercourse with one another.*"[35]

Freud was quick to acknowledge that his was not the orthodox view. Indeed among anthropologists there was no single accepted account of totemism. Everything connected with it, Freud wrote, "seems to be puzzling: the decisive problems concern the origin of the idea of descent from the totem and the reasons for exogamy (or rather for the taboo upon incest of which exogamy is the expression), as well as the relation between the two institutions, totemic organization and prohibition against incest." Still, he had a clear notion of what was required for a satisfactory explanation: it "should be at once a historical and a psychological one. It should tell us under what conditions this peculiar institution developed and to what psychical needs" it has given voice.[36]

At this point Freud reviewed theories about totemism, about exogamy, and about the relation or non-relation between the two. He came away dissatisfied and expected his readers to feel disappointed as well. He thus prepared his audience for one last effort:

> This attempt is based upon a hypothesis of Charles Darwin's. . . ."[T]he most probable view is that primaeval man aboriginally lived in small communities [or hordes], each with as many wives as he could support and obtain, whom he would have . . . guarded against all other men. Or he may have lived with several wives by himself, like the Gorilla; for all the natives 'agree that but one adult male is seen in a band; when the young male grows up, a contest takes place for mastery, and the strongest, by killing and driving out the others, establishes himself as the head of the community.' The younger males, being thus expelled and wandering about, would, when at last successful in finding a partner, prevent too close interbreeding within the limits of the same family."[37]

How Darwin's primal horde could resolve the outstanding anthropological riddles was not immediately apparent. To be sure exogamy for young males was implicit in his story: after all, there was "a violent and jealous father" keeping "all the females to himself," driving "away his sons" as they reached manhood.[38] But the relation between it and totemism remained obscure. Indeed totemism itself found no place in Darwin's tale. In this fashion Freud located deficiencies that, thanks to his psychoanalytic experience, he felt in a position to remedy.

*   *   *

Freud drew on what he had learned about children's relations to animals. Like primitives, he claimed, they "have no scruples over allowing animals to rank as their full equals. Uninhibited as they are in their bodily needs, they no doubt feel themselves more akin to animals than to their elders." Yet "not infrequently . . . a strange rift occurs. . . . A child will suddenly begin to be frightened of some particular species of animal and to avoid touching or seeing any individual of that species."[39] So it had been with Little Hans. The son of Max Graf, a musicologist and member of Freud's first psychoanalytic group, the Wednesday Psychological Society, he was analyzed by his father with Freud serving as consultant and/or supervisor.

Graf and his wife – she herself had fallen "ill with a neurosis . . . during her girlhood" and had been treated by Freud – had agreed to experiment with letting their son "grow and express himself without being intimidated. . . . They would use no more coercion than might be absolutely necessary for maintaining good behaviour." Yet in two respects the parents adhered more closely to prevailing cultural practices than to Freudian precepts in the making. When Hans was 3½ – the reporting on this "cheerful, . . . active-minded young fellow" began when he was 3 – his mother "found him with his hand on his penis" and threatened to summon the doctor to cut off his "wiwi-maker." At about the same age a sister was born, and to prepare for "the great event of Hans's life," his parents trotted out the fable of the stork. Shortly before the boy turned 5, the tenor of the reporting changed. He had started "setting . . . problems" for his parents, and the material his father now sent was "material for a case history."[40]

What was the matter with Hans? One day on his way to the public gardens with his nursemaid for his regular outing, he was overcome by anxiety; he began to cry and asked to return home to the comfort of his mother. When questioned, he could not say what he was afraid of. The next day his mother accompanied him; again the anxiety proved overwhelming, forcing him to take refuge in the house. When questioned once more, "after much internal struggling," he replied: "*I was afraid a horse would bite me.*" This was the first content of Hans's disorder, which Freud classified as a phobia; it was not the last.

> He was not only afraid of horses biting him . . . but also of carts, furniture-vans, and of buses . . ., and of horses that started moving, of horses that looked big and heavy, and of horses that drove quickly. . . . [H]e was afraid of horses *falling down*, and consequently incorporated in his phobia everything that seemed to facilitate their falling down.[41]

Even before the onset of his phobia, Hans had displayed the principal trait of his sexual life: "a quite peculiarly lively interest in his wiwi-maker." The boy's "Weltanschauung" first came to the notice of his attentive father on trips to the zoo. "Standing in front of the lion's cage . . . Hans called out in a joyful and excited voice: 'I can see the lion's wiwi-maker.'" When his father drew a picture of a giraffe, the boy complained that its genital organ was not visible. "Draw its wiwi-maker too," he insisted. "Draw it yourself," the father answered. Hans complied with a short line, then extended it until it was almost the length of the animal's leg. When the father and son walked past a horse that was urinating, Hans commented: "The horse has got its wiwi-maker underneath like me." And one time when he was at the railroad station and "saw water being let out of an engine," he remarked: "Oh look . . . the engine is making wiwi." Not long thereafter he formulated the crucial difference between animate and inanimate, therewith recognizing that he had made a mistake: "A dog and a horse have wiwi-makers, a table and a chair haven't."[42]

In the course of the analysis the father provided much in the way of enlightenment. It did not extend to sexual intercourse. (Freud thought that the "educational experiment" had not been carried far enough: the boy should have been told about the "existence of the vagina and of copulation.")[43] Still Hans had inklings. Witness a fantasy he reported to his father: "I was with you at Schönbrun [the location of the zoo] where the sheep are; and then we crawled through under the ropes, and then . . . the policemen . . . grabbed hold of us." Hans also remembered having thought something, something forbidden: "I went with you in the train, and we smashed a window and the policeman took us off with him." The fantasies, Freud noted, offered "certain pictorial representations" for a "vague notion . . . of something that he might do with his mother," something, Hans seemed to be saying, "I do not know what it is, but I do know that you [the father] are doing it too." The boy did not always imagine the father playing such a benign role. In a further fantasy Hans offered a different version of what he did with his mother and of his father's attitude to it: "*In the night there was a big giraffe in the room and a crumpled one; and the big one called out because I took the crumpled one away from it. Then it stopped calling out, and then I sat down on top of the crumpled one.*" The big giraffe was himself, the father wrote Freud – and Freud agreed – or rather his "big penis (the long neck)" and the crumpled giraffe was his wife, "or rather her genital organ."

The whole thing is a reproduction of a scene which has been gone through almost every morning for the last few days. Hans always comes to us in the early morning, and my wife cannot resist taking him into bed with her for a few minutes. Thereupon I always warn her not to . . . ("the big one called out because I'd taken the crumpled one away from it"); and she answers now and then, rather irritated, no doubt, that it's all nonsense, that after all one minute is of no importance, and so on. Then Hans stays with her a little while. ("Then the big one stopped calling out, and then I sat down on top of the crumpled one.")[44]

Two days later the father took Hans to see Freud. It was the only time during the treatment that Freud saw the boy.

> I already knew the funny little fellow, and with all his self-assurance he was yet so amiable that I had always been glad to see him. I do not know whether he remembered me, but he behaved irreproachably and like a perfectly reasonable member of human society. The consultation was a short one. His father opened it by remarking that, in spite of all the pieces of enlightenment we had given Hans, his fear of horses had not yet diminished. . . . Certain details which I now learnt – to the effect that he was particularly bothered by what horses wear in front of their eyes and by the black around their mouths – were . . . not to be explained from what we knew. But as I saw the two of them sitting in front of me and at the same time heard Hans's description of his anxiety-horses, a further piece of the solution shot through my mind, and a piece which I could well understand might escape his father. I asked Hans jokingly whether his horses wore eyeglasses, to which he replied that they did not. I then asked him whether his father wore eyeglasses, to which, against all the evidence, he once more said no. Finally I asked him whether by "the black around the mouth" he meant a moustache; and I then disclosed to him that he was afraid of his father, . . . because he was so fond of his mother. . . . Long before he came into the world, I went on, I had known that a little Hans would come who would be so fond of his mother that he would be bound to feel afraid of his father because of it.

It now became clear: "The horse must be his father."[45] Here, Freud remarked in *Totem and Taboo*, was "a fact with an important bearing on totemism": under the sway of the Oedipus complex – and Hans stood as a prime example of a "little Oedipus" – "children displace some of their feelings from the father on to an animal."[46]

And so Freud arrived at the conclusion that "the totemic system . . . was a product of the conditions involved in the Oedipus complex." The "two principal ordinances of totemism, the two taboo prohibitions which constitute its core – not to kill the totem and not to have sexual relations with a woman of the same totem – coincide with the two crimes of Oedipus . . . as well as with the two primal wishes of [male] children."[47] Freud now possessed a psychological explanation of totemism; a historical one still eluded him. Until he had both, he would be unable to complete Darwin's tale of the primal horde.

*   *   *

On September 21, 1897 Freud had written his great friend Wilhelm Fliess confiding "the great secret" that in "the last few months" had been "slowly dawning";[48] he no longer believed his explanation of hysteria – an explanation that became known as the seduction hypothesis. In framing that hypothesis Freud had invited history into the unconscious domain; in retreating from it he had no intention of rescinding his invitation. Historical reality might be difficult to uncover; but he was determined to continue his excavation.[49]

> *[O]ur hysterical patients suffer from reminiscences.* Their symptoms are residues and mnemic symbols of particular (traumatic) experiences. . . . The monuments and memorials with which large cities are adorned are also mnemic symbols. If you take a walk through the streets of London, you will find in front of one of the great railway termini, a richly carved Gothic column – Charing Cross. One of the old Plantagenet kings of the thirteenth century ordered the body of his beloved Queen Eleanor to be carried to Westminster; and at every stage at which the coffin rested he erected a Gothic Cross. Charing Cross is the last of the monuments that commemorate the funeral cortège. . . . [W]hat should we think of a Londoner who paused to-day in deep melancholy before the memorial of Queen Eleanor's funeral instead of going about his business in the hurry that modern working conditions demand or instead of feeling joy over the youthful queen of his own heart? Yet every single hysteric . . . behaves like . . . [such an unpractical Londoner].[50]

In *Totem and Taboo* Freud continued his quest for the historical past. He proceeded as was his wont with hysterical patients, that is, retrospectively, starting from the monument or memorial that served as a mnemic symbol. In his study of totemism he fastened on ritual sacrifice and on William Robertson-Smith's interpretation of it as "sacramental killing and communal eating of the totem animal."[51] Freud elaborated; he drew a verbal picture of an imaginary totem meal:

> The clan is celebrating the ceremonial occasion by the cruel slaughter of its totem animal and is devouring it raw – blood, flesh and bones. The clansmen are there, dressed in the likeness of the totem and imitating it in sound and movement, as though they are seeking to stress their identity with it. Each man is conscious that he is performing an act forbidden to the individual and justifiable only through the participation of the whole clan; nor may anyone absent himself from the killing and the meal. Then the deed is done, the slaughtered animal is lamented and bewailed. The mourning is obligatory, imposed by dread of a threatened retribution. . . .
> [T]he mourning is followed by demonstrations of festive rejoicing; every instinct is unfettered and there is license for every kind of

gratification. . . . [E]xcess is of the essence of a festival; the festive feeling is produced by the liberty to do what is as a rule prohibited.[52]

What, then, did the totem meal memorialize? Recall Darwin's hypothesis of the primal horde and Freud's determination to find a place for totemism in it. Recall also Freud's speculation – or, rather, assertion – that the totem animal was in reality a substitute for the hated – and loved – father. Freud drew another imaginary scene:

> One day the brothers who had been driven out came together, killed and devoured their father and so made an end of the patriarchal horde. United, they had the courage to do and succeeded in doing what would have been impossible for them individually. . . . Cannibal savages as they were, it goes without saying that they devoured their victim as well as killing him. The violent primal father had doubtless been the feared and envied model of each one of the . . . brothers; and in the act of devouring him . . ., each one of them acquired a portion of his strength. The totem meal . . . would thus be a repetition and commemoration of this memorable and criminal deed.

That was not all. After the brothers had murdered their father, after they had satisfied their hatred of him, their affection, "which had all this time been pushed under, was bound to make itself felt":

> It did so in the form of remorse. . . . What had up to then been prevented by his [the father's] actual existence was thenceforward prohibited by the sons themselves. . . . They revoked their deed by forbidding the killing of the totem, the substitute for their father; and they renounced its fruits by resigning their claim to the women who had now been set free. . . . Whoever contravened these taboos became guilty of the only two crimes with which primitive society concerned itself.

And so Freud reached the conclusion that "totemism and exogamy were intimately connected and had a simultaneous origin."[53]

Note that together with remorse, "a sense of guilt made its appearance." Note too its derivation from "the *affectionate* current of feeling towards the father."[54] This affectionate current, Freud was suggesting, created genuine moral sensibilities.

*   *   *

Were the primal horde and the primal crime mere figures of speech or were they historical actualities? Down to his very last book, Freud maintained that he had written of a historical event, albeit many times repeated. Even the realization that this claim entailed a further claim – that "the sense of guilt for an action . . . persisted for many thousands of years and . . . remained operative in generations which . . . had no knowledge of that action" – did not shake him.[55] His insistence reinstated a sharp dichotomy between historical and psychical reality – a dichotomy that his formulation of the Oedipus complex had called into question.

This same insistence prompted Freud to "examine more closely the case of neurosis." After all neurotics, particularly obsessional neurotics, had a powerful sense of guilt; they also had "impulses and emotions, set upon evil ends but held back from their achievement." Were there really no deeds? Were neurotics "defending themselves only against *psychical* reality and . . . punishing themselves for impulses which were merely *felt*"? Historical reality, Freud argued, had a share as well. "In their childhood they had these evil impulses pure and simple, and turned them into acts so far as the impotence of childhood allowed. Each of these excessively virtuous individuals passed through an evil period in his infancy – a phase of perversion which was the forerunner and precondition of the later period of excessive morality." Freud thus chose to play down what he had learned from Ernst Lanzer about the omnipotence of thoughts; he opted instead to end on a rhetorical note: "[I]n the beginning was the Deed."[56]

Coda: "Criminals from a Sense of Guilt"

In the briefest of the three studies that make up "Some Character-Types Met with in Psycho-Analytic Work" (1916), Freud identified what he called "criminals from a sense of guilt." He arrived at this formula initially from accounts by "very respectable" patients of "forbidden actions" that they had engaged in when young – "such as thefts, frauds and even arson" – and subsequently "from a more thorough study of . . . cases in which the misdeeds were committed" when the patients were mature and in treatment with him. Analytic work then brought the surprising discovery that the execution of these actions "was accompanied by mental relief" for the perpetrator. He had been "suffering from an oppressive feeling of guilt" – of unknown origin – and after the deed was done, "this oppression was mitigated. His sense of guilt was at least attached to something."[57]

As to its cause, Freud invoked the Oedipus complex: the guilt was "a reaction to the two great criminal intentions of killing the father and having sexual relations with the mother." He also introduced the argument of *Totem and Taboo*:

> We must remember . . . that parricide and incest with the mother are the two great human crimes, the only ones which, as such, are pursued and abhorred in primitive communities. And we must remember, too, how close other investigations have brought us to the hypothesis that

the conscience of mankind, which now appears as an inherited mental force, was acquired in connection with the Oedipus complex.[58]

Recall, the Oedipus complex belongs to the unconscious. So too does "the heritage of emotion . . . left behind by the original relation to the father."[59] It follows – whether looked at ontogenetically or phylogenetically – that "a great part of the sense of guilt must . . . remain unconscious."[60] It follows as well that man is far more guilt-ridden than he knows.

*   *   *

What are the themes that I want to highlight for future reference? Three stand out. They were part of Klein's Freudian inheritance and were elaborated by her and her followers.

First: omnipotence of thoughts. In Klein's hands it became omnipotence of fantasy – which she spelled with a *ph* to indicate imaginative activity underlying all thought and feeling as opposed to simply fancying or whimsical speculation.[61] The philosopher Richard Wollheim read "Criminals from a Sense of Guilt" accordingly. It – the sense of guilt – could be traced "back to the incestuous and murderous wishes *omnipotently* entertained at the height of the Oedipal phase. That these wishes were *omnipotently* entertained is significant": it means that for the adult agent there is scant, if any, appreciation "of the fact that the objects of his wishes were things that he had merely desired as opposed to things that he had actually done. And given the enormity of these things – sexual intercourse with the mother, dismemberment and destruction of the father – it is . . . [hardly] surprising that the aspirant criminal could feel that any crime he contemplated was barely a match for the guilt that already tormented him."[62] There was no chance that Kleinians – and Wollheim was much influenced by Klein – would disregard the lesson that Ernst Lanzer had taught.

Second: ambivalence. In March 1912 Freud reported to Carl Gustav Jung: "My paper on Taboo is coming slowly. The conclusion has long been known to me. The source of taboo and hence also of conscience is ambivalence."[63] In "Criminals from a Sense of Guilt" he claimed that conscience was "acquired in connection with the Oedipus complex."[64] The two statements could be reconciled: after all, it was "with their father-complex" that "psychoanalytic examination of modern individuals" found ambivalence "at its strongest."[65] That moral sensibilities derived from ambivalence would be a key feature of Klein's thinking.

Third: the inescapability of guilt. Given his claims about the primal crime and an "inherited mental force," Freud would seem to have committed himself to guilt being unavoidable – at least in males. In fact, he hedged on this point: he allowed for a minority of criminals who "commit crimes without any sense of guilt, who have either developed no moral inhibitions or who, in their conflict with society, consider themselves justified in their action."[66] Klein disagreed. She wrote about a 12-year-old boy already started on a criminal career: "[H]is feeling of guilt drove him to repeat again and again acts which were to be punished by a cruel father or mother, or even both. His apparent indifference to punishment, his apparent lack of fear were completely misleading."[67] Klein had only 14 sessions with the boy and hence had not time enough to attempt the task she was setting herself: to uncover or recover the guilt that to all intents and purposes had gone missing and to explain how it had been warded off and/or defended against.

Chapter 2

Reparation gone awry

Even at the time it was published, *Totem and Taboo* (1913) struck those who were not Freud's loyal adherents as fanciful – "a 'Just-So Story,' as it was amusingly called by a not unkind English critic." Despite the bad review – by the anthropologist Robert R. Marett – Freud held fast to his hypothesis, and in Chapter 10 of *Group Psychology and the Analysis of the Ego* (1921), he returned to it.

> In 1912 I took up the conjecture of Darwin's to the effect that the primitive form of human society was that of a horde ruled over despotically by a powerful male. I attempted to show that the fortunes of this horde have left indestructible traces upon the history of human descent; and, especially, that the development of totemism, which comprises in itself the beginnings of religion, morality, and social organization, is connected with the killing of the chief by violence and the transformation of the paternal horde into a community of brothers.

Resorting again to conjecture, he proposed a simple equation: group equals primal horde. "The group," he claimed, could be regarded "as a revival of the primal horde. Just as primitive man survives potentially in every individual, so the primal horde may arise once more out of any random collection."[1] In this fashion, the present might provide clues to the prehistoric.

Freud's immediate followers showed little interest in renewing the quest for the primeval. One example: Sándor Ferenczi, who had participated with Freud in many a phylogenetic excursion, emphasized the "respects in which Freud's dissection of the group mind" helped explain "the normal and pathological psychology of the individual."[2] Another: Ernest Jones laid stress on Freud's "new ideas about the psychology of the ego" and more specifically on his account of the relations between ego and ego ideal.[3] My interests are similar to those of Ferenczi and Jones. Once again I intend to set aside the anthropological in favor of the psychological – and the ethical as well.

Curiously enough, ambivalence, so central in *Totem and Taboo*, was largely missing from *Group Psychology*. Ferenczi questioned Freud on this point. "Should not *ambivalence*," he asked, "be brought into relation with the beginning formation of the ego ideal?"[4] By the same token, guilt was not much in evidence. Given that an affectionate current of feeling awakened guilt and/or remorse only after a hostile current had been acted upon, how could it have been otherwise? No ambivalence, no guilt.

Why, then, bother to discuss *Group Psychology*? Because Melanie Klein expanded on those "new ideas about the psychology of the ego." She did so in two major ways. In the first instance she enlarged upon the process by which an ego ideal (Freud's term) or a good object (Klein's term) came to be an internal authority; she enlarged on it to usher in her notion of a complex internal object world. In the second instance she gave an account of the relations between ego and ego ideal or rather ego and internal objects – summed up in her concept of the depressive position – in which ambivalence returned to center stage. And with ambivalence, along came guilt.

And a further question as well: how might the guilt Klein described be assuaged? Reparation was the answer she gave. Very early in her career she noted the violence and cruelty with which children dealt with their objects – and the remorse and concern that ensued.

> [T]he impression I get of the way in which even the quite small child fights his unsocial tendencies is rather touching. . . . A manifestation of primitive tendencies is invariably followed by anxiety, and by performances which show how the child now tries to make good and atone for what . . . [she] has done. Sometimes . . . [she] tries to mend the very same . . . [toy figures], trains and so on . . . [she] has just broken. Sometimes drawing, building and so on express the same reactive tendencies.[5]

But attempts at reparation could go awry – indeed frequently they did. Klein's close associate, Joan Riviere, explored such a derailment by way of Henrik Ibsen's play *The Master Builder*. She adopted a practice, not uncommon among psychoanalysts, least of all Freud himself, of turning to literary examples to represent, in dramatic fashion, psychoanalytic concepts – in this instance manic defenses against guilt.

Group Psychology and the Analysis of the Ego

What is the nature of the mental changes that a group forces upon an individual? Gustav Le Bon posed this question, and Freud took his cue from him. "The most striking peculiarity," the Frenchman answered, "is the following":

> Whoever be the individuals that compose it, however like or unlike be
> their mode of life, their occupations, their character, or their intelli-
> gence, the fact that they have been transformed into a group puts them
> in possession of a sort of collective mind which makes them feel, think,
> and act in a manner quite different from that in which each individual
> of them would feel, think, and act were he in a state of isolation.

To account for this blotting out of an individual's "particular acquire-
ments," he pointed to hypnotic influence and/or suggestion.

> The most careful investigations seem to prove that an individual
> immersed for some length of time in a group in action soon finds
> himself . . . in a special state, which much resembles the state of . . . the
> hypnotized individual . . . in the hands of the hypnotizer. . . . Under the
> influence of a suggestion, he will undertake the accomplishment of
> certain acts of irresistible impetuosity. This impetuosity is the more
> irresistible in the case of groups than in that of the hypnotized subject,
> from the fact that, suggestion being the same for all the individuals in
> the group, it gains in strength by reciprocity.[6]

So far, so good; but what about the person who in the case of a group took
the place of the hypnotist?

By the time Freud had finished with Le Bon and some lesser figures, his
own project had acquired two complementary foci: the ties that bound a
group together and the role a leader played in cementing those ties.

*   *   *

The discussion of hypnotic influence brought Freud back to his first
psychoanalytic cases, to the time when he had made use of it to gain access
to the warded off memories of his hysterical patients. In 1889, to hone his
technique, he had taken the trouble of visiting Nancy to study with
Hippolyte Bernheim. In his *Studies on Hysteria* (1893–1895), authored
jointly with Josef Breuer, only one of his cases, that of Emmy von N.,
benefitted from the trip. With Elisabeth von R. and again with Lucy, Freud
discovered that his powers as a hypnotist had "severe limits." So he turned
to "concentration" combined with "pressure."[7] And then between the time
he worked with Lucy and the time he treated Dora, the patient described in
the "Fragment of an Analysis of a Case of Hysteria" (1905), psychoanalytic
technique was "completely revolutionized."

> Without exerting any . . . kind of influence, he [the analyst] invites them
> [the patients] to lie down in a comfortable attitude on a sofa, while he
> himself sits on a chair behind them outside their field of vision. He does
> not even ask them to close their eyes, and avoids touching them in any

way, as well as any other procedure which might be reminiscent of hypnosis. The session thus proceeds like a conversation between two people equally awake, but one of whom is spared every muscular exertion and every disturbing sensory impression which might divert his attention from his own mental activity.[8]

By the time Freud wrote up Dora's case, he had not only abandoned hypnotism; he had also come to appreciate that hypnotic suggestion itself did not constitute bedrock – it was not irreducible.

As early as *Studies on Hysteria* Freud recognized that he – and his then much-prized pressure technique – risked defeat if "distressing ideas" arising "from the content of the analysis" were "transferred on to the figure of the analyst." He gave an example:

> In one of my patients the origin of a particular hysterical symptom lay in a wish, which she had had many years earlier and had at once relegated to the unconscious, that the man she was talking to at the time might boldly take the initiative and give her a kiss. On one occasion, at the end of a session, a similar wish came up in her about me. She was horrified at it, spent a sleepless night, and at the next session, though she did not refuse to be treated, was quite useless for work. After I had discovered the obstacle and removed it, the work proceeded further.[9]

In the postscript to "Fragment of an Analysis," Freud spelled out at greater length what he meant.

> What are transferences? They are new editions or facsimiles of the impulses and phantasies which are aroused and made conscious during the progress of the analysis; but they have this peculiarity, which is characteristic for their species, that they replace some earlier person with the person of the physician. To put it another way: a whole series of psychological experiences are revived, not as belonging to the past, but as applying to the person of the physician at the present moment. Some of the transferences have a content which differs from that of their model in no respect whatever except for the substitution. These then – to keep to the same metaphor – are merely new impressions or reprints. Others are more ingeniously constructed; their content has been subjected to a moderating influence . . . and they . . . become conscious . . . by cleverly taking advantage of some real peculiarity in the physician's person or circumstances and attaching themselves to that. These, then, will no longer be new impressions, but revised editions.[10]

Transference obviously trumped suggestion: "*[T]he capacity to be hypnotised and influenced by suggestion depends on the possibility of transference taking place.*"[11] The words are Ferenczi's; but the thought comes from Freud.

*   *   *

Freud pressed on: suggestion rested on transference; transference, in turn, rested on libido.

> Libido is an expression taken from the theory of the emotions. We call by that name the energy, regarded as a quantitative magnitude (though not at this point actually measurable), of those instincts which have to do with all that may be comprised under the word "love." The nucleus of what we mean by love naturally consists (and this is what is commonly called love, and what the poets sing of) in sexual love with sexual union as its aim. But we do not separate from this – what in any case has a share in the name "love" – on the one-hand, self-love, and on the other, love for parents and children, friendship and love for humanity in general, and also devotion to concrete objects and to abstract ideas. Our justification lies in the fact that psycho-analytic research has taught us that all these tendencies are an expression of the same instinctual impulses; in relations between the sexes these impulses force their way toward sexual union, but in other circumstances they are diverted from this aim or are prevented from reaching it, though always preserving enough of their original nature to keep their identity recognizable (as in such features as longing for proximity, and self-sacrifice).[12]

With the invocation of libido, Freud recalled the questions he had initially posed. Had he settled the first question, that is, what power holds the group together, what power prompts the individual to give up his distinctiveness? Was it the case that "concealed behind the shelter, the screen of suggestion" – so that "the authorities" had failed to detect their presence – lay "love relationships"? Did they make a group cohere? Did they constitute "the essence of the group mind"?[13]

*   *   *

Without answering, Freud turned to his second question, namely, the leader's contribution to group solidarity. At this point he brought into the discussion and compared two apparently dissimilar institutions: the church and the army. In both there is "a head – in the Church Christ, in an army its Commander-in-Chief – who, so it is claimed, loves all the individuals in the group with an equal love."

This equal love was expressly enunciated by Christ: "Inasmuch as ye have done it unto the least of my brethren, ye have done it unto me." . . . All the demands that are made upon the individual are derived from this love of Christ's. . . . It is not without deep reason that the similarity between the Christian community and a family is invoked, and that believers call themselves brothers in Christ, that is, brothers through the love that Christ has for them.

And thus too with an army:

The Commander-in-Chief is a father who loves all soldiers equally, and for that reason they are comrades among themselves. . . . Every captain is, as it were, the Commander-in-Chief and the father of his company, and so is every non-commissioned officer of his section.[14]

Libidinal ties are notoriously volatile; with regard to the church and the army, they were deceptive as well. The notion that Christ or the Commander-in-Chief loved all the individuals in the group with equal love, Freud considered an illusion; but "if it were to be dropped, then both Church and army would dissolve, so far as . . . external force permitted."[15]

Freud had taken up two questions; yet in neither instance had he fully fathomed the binding attachments at work. He said to himself, in effect, that choosing an object and loving it, whether or not the sexual aim be inhibited, must not represent "the only manner of emotional tie with other people."[16]

*   *   *

Here Freud introduced two concepts: identification and the ego ideal. With these terms in place or, better, in play, relations between followers and leader and among the followers themselves could be readily schematized.

Identification came in many forms. In "Fragment of an Analysis," in connection with Dora's cough and aphonia, Freud mentioned two of them. The cough had first become troublesome, along with migraine headaches, when the girl was 12. Before she encountered Freud the migraines had grown less frequent and had then vanished altogether. Not so the attacks of *tussis nervosa*. Freud assumed that the "presence of a real and organically determined irritation of the throat . . . acted like that grain of sand around which an oyster forms its pearl." Elsewhere he dispensed with metaphor and simply claimed that the nervous cough "had no doubt been started by a common catarrh."[17] What meanings, he wondered, had Dora attached to the physical irritation?

In the first instance Dora's attacks of coughing and accompanying aphonia mimicked the behavior of her father's mistress, Frau K. Whenever her husband was away, Frau K. felt fine; whenever he returned, she suddenly fell ill. She was obviously using ill-health to avoid "conjugal duties," and the presence or absence of her husband had a decisive "influence upon the appearance and disappearance of the symptoms of her illness." This much Freud had surmised – and his patient had as well. Might not Dora's health be determined in a similar fashion – or rather, in reverse: she was well when Herr K. was present, ill when he was absent? (Freud had already come to the conclusion that Dora secretly loved Herr K.) Freud asked his patient what the average length of her attacks of aphonia had been:

> "From three to six weeks, perhaps." How long had Herr K.'s absences lasted? "Three to six weeks, too," she was obliged to admit. Her illness was therefore a demonstration of her love for K., just as his wife's was a demonstration of her *dislike*.

How could Dora's illness serve as such a demonstration? "When the man she loved was away," Freud interpreted, "she gave up speaking; speech had lost its value since she could not speak to him."[18] (Freud did not report Dora's response to his interpretation.) This kind of identification, Freud wrote in *Group Psychology*, rested on the possibility of putting oneself in a situation comparable to that of the other person. "[I]t may arise with any new perception of a common quality. . . . The more important this common quality is, the more successful may this partial identification become, and it thus may represent the beginning of a new tie."[19]

In the second instance Dora's cough was "an imitation of her father (whose lungs were affected), and could serve as an expression of her sympathy and concern for him."[20] In *Group Psychology* he elaborated. Dora and her cough now figured as an example of an identification that appeared *instead* of an object choice. At this point Freud introduced a distinction – between identification and object choice – that he had come to appreciate only after he had written "Fragment of an Analysis."

> Identification is known to psycho-analysis as the earliest expression of an emotional tie to another person. It plays a part in the early history of the Oedipus complex. A little boy will exhibit a special interest in his father; he would like to grow like him and be like him, and take his place everywhere. . . . At the same time as this identification with his father, or a little later, the boy has begun to develop a true object-relation towards his mother. . . . He then exhibits, therefore, two psychologically distinct ties: a straightforward sexual object-cathexis towards his mother and an identification with his father which takes him as his model. The two subsist side by side for a time without any mutual influence or interference. In consequence of the irresistible advance towards a unification of mental life, they come together at last; and the normal Oedipus complex originates from their confluence. The little boy notices that the father stands in his way with his mother.

With Dora and her father, Freud was not pointing to an original identification. Rather:

> [I]t often happens that under the conditions in which symptoms are constructed, that is, where there is repression and where the mechanisms of the unconscious are dominant, object-choice is turned back into identification – the ego assumes the characteristics of the object.

Freud summed up: identification "becomes a substitute for a libidinal object-tie, as it were by means of introjection of the object into the ego."[21]

Note the "as it were." Freud admitted his difficulty in providing a "clear metapsychological representation."[22] In "Mourning and Melancholia" (1917) he had written of an object-relationship being shattered, of the ego's identification with the abandoned object, its introjection of the lost object, and – as a result – the "shadow of the object" falling on the ego.[23] In *Leonardo Da Vinci and a Memory of His Childhood* (1910) Freud had described the artist's intense fixation on his mother, his failure to find an erotic substitute for her, his putting himself in her place: he loved boys the way his mother had "loved *him* when he was a child"; his pupils selected not for their talent but for their beauty, "he treated . . . with kindness and consideration, looked after them, and when they were ill nursed them himself, . . . just as his mother might have tended him."[24] In this case a smile, not a shadow, had fallen upon the ego.

Freud moved on to a second crucial concept – the ego ideal – and he did so with Leonardo very much in mind. In caring for his pupils, Leonardo was taking "his own person as a model" for the "new objects of his love": the boys whom he now loved were surrogate "figures and revivals of himself in childhood."[25] He was searching for his "own childhood ego."[26] In "On Narcissism: An Introduction" (1914) Freud continued in similar vein:

> As always where the libido is concerned, man has . . . again shown himself incapable of giving up a satisfaction he has once enjoyed. He is not willing to forgo the narcissistic perfection of his childhood; and when, as he grows up, he is disturbed by the admonitions of others and by the awakening of his own critical judgement, so that he can no longer retain that perfection, he seeks to recover it in the new form of an ego ideal. What he projects before him as his ideal is the substitute for the lost narcissism of his childhood.[27]

Freud ended the paper with another step: he soldered together – without fanfare – the ego ideal and conscience.[28] Then in *Group Psychology* he treated this soldering together as well-established.

> [B]y way of functions we have ascribed to it [the ego ideal] self-observation, the moral conscience, the censorship of dreams, and the

chief influence in repression. We have said that it is the heir to the original narcissism in which the childish ego enjoyed self-sufficiency; it gradually gathers up from the influences of the environment the demands which that environment makes upon the ego and which the ego cannot always rise to; so that a man, when he cannot be satisfied with his ego itself, may nevertheless be able to find satisfaction in the ego ideal which has been differentiated out of the ego.[29]

Freud was now ready to return to the "riddle of the group."

[A]fter the preceding discussions we are quite in a position to give the formula for the libidinal constitution of groups, or at least of such groups as we have hitherto considered – namely, those that have a leader. . . . *A group of this kind is a number of individuals who have put one and the same object in the place of their ego ideal and have consequently identified themselves with one another in their ego.*

In other words, the emotional link within the group derived from, and was sustained by, the link between the group and its leader. And so it has been since time immemorial: "*[M]an* is . . . a horde animal, an individual creature in a horde led by a chief."[30]

*   *   *

Recall the appearance of remorse in *Totem and Taboo*. It followed upon the primal crime: after the brothers had murdered their father, after they had satisfied their hatred of him, their affection re-emerged and, along with it, a sense of guilt. Neither ambivalence nor guilt has yet come into my discussion of *Group Psychology*.

Let me start with ambivalence. It is noticeable by its absence. Just when the reader would expect Freud to bring it in, he deflects it or rather suggests that the group deflects it:

We have seen that with an army and a Church . . . the contrivance by means of which an artificial group is held together . . . is the illusion that the leader loves all of the individuals equally and justly. But this is simply an idealistic remodelling of the state of affairs in the primal horde, where all the sons knew that they were equally *persecuted* by the primal father, and *feared* him equally.

Idealistic or idealizing? Having been put in the place of the ego ideal, it stood to reason that the leader would inherit the love earlier bestowed on that ideal: "a considerable amount of narcissistic libido" would overflow onto the leader.[31] First the ego ideal and then the leader was thought to possess every perfection. This idealization denied hostility; it kept hostility forcibly at bay. And no ambivalence, no guilt.

Let me move on to Freud's remarks about guilt itself. In *Totem and Taboo* Freud's thinking about guilt was not particularly theoretical. In *Group Psychology*, having introduced the ego ideal, Freud construed the sense of guilt "as an expression of the tension between the ego and the ego ideal." The tension – "the renunciations and limitations imposed upon the ego" – could not be borne without complaint. Relief or release was in order:

> The Saturnalia of the Romans and our modern carnival . . . [as well as] the festivals of primitive people . . . usually end in debaucheries of every kind and the transgression of what are at other times the most sacred commandments. . . . [T]he abrogation of the ideal would necessarily be a magnificent festival for the ego.

Freud likened this abrogation to mania:

> [I]t cannot be doubted that in cases of mania the ego and ego ideal have fused together, so that the person, in a mood of triumph and self-satisfaction, disturbed by no self-criticism, can enjoy the abolition of his inhibitions, his feelings of consideration for others, and his self-reproaches.[32]

And his sense of guilt as well.

Klein cited *Group Psychology* in her own writings only once.[33] Yet she picked up right from where Freud left off. The introjection of an object, Freud claimed allowed "the interplay between the external object and the ego" to be repeated upon a "new scene of action within the ego."[34] In Klein's hands this new scene of action became an inner world of complex object relations – rife with love, hate, and guilt.

To the depressive position

In 1943 and 1944 the British Psycho-Analytical Society held a series of scientific meetings devoted to examining theoretical disputes – a series that came to be known as the Controversial Discussions. The controversy had been simmering since the mid-1930s when Klein first outlined her notion of the depressive position. It came to a boil after 1938 with the arrival in London of Anna Freud and other émigrés from central Europe. Finding herself on the defensive, Klein agreed to "make it clear in what respects . . . [her] views . . . either amplified accepted Freudian teaching" or called "for a modification of it."[35] In this endeavor she was joined by Paula Heimann and Susan Isaacs, with Heimann's paper, "Some Aspects of the Role of

Introjection and Projection in Early Development" – the second in the series – the subject of the meeting on October 20, 1943.[36]

Heimann took off from Freud's essay "Negation" (1925). She used it to introduce the species of fantasy, introjection and projection, that for her, as for Klein, occupied "a special place in the building up of the structure of the mind."[37] According to Freud:

> The function of judgement . . . affirms or disaffirms the possession by a thing of a particular attribute. . . . The attribute to be decided about may originally have been good or bad, useful or harmful. Expressed in the language of the oldest – the oral – instinctual impulses, the judgement is: "I should like to eat this," or "I should like to spit it out"; and put more generally: "I should like to take this into myself and to keep that out." That is to say: "It shall be inside me" or "it shall be outside me.". . . [T]he original pleasure ego wants to introject into itself everything that is good and to eject everything that is bad.[38]

Heimann added:

> The mind . . . achieves adaptation and progress by employing through-out its existence the fundamental and basic processes of introjection and projection. . . . Such taking in and expelling consists of an active interplay between the organism and the outer world; on this funda-mental pattern rests all intercourse between subject and object. I believe that in the last analysis we may find it at bottom of all of our complicated dealings with one another.[39]

Here Heimann linked introjection and projection to early object relations, that is, to the earliest relations between self and other, which Klein insisted started "from the beginning of post-natal life"[40] – and not with the phallic stage, as Anna Freud claimed. And here too Heimann turned to Freud, to his paper "Mourning and Melancholia" (1917). In it Freud had talked of identification being modeled on introjection or oral incorporation; he had considered it a "regression to . . . the oral phase" aimed at "a setting up of the object inside the ego." In *The Ego and the Id* (1923) he suggested that identification/introjection was not restricted to mourning or melancholia. Freud wrote:

> [T]he process, "especially in the early phase of development, is a very frequent one, and it makes it possible to suppose that the character of the ego is a precipitate of abandoned object-cathexes and that it con-tains a history of those object-choices."[41]

Heimann chimed in and elaborated. "We assume that during the first few months of life there exists in phantasy a 'good' breast side by side with a 'bad' breast, and . . . introjection and projection . . . work in a relatively simple manner: the 'good' breast is introjected and kept inside, the 'bad' breast projected." Whether simple or not – and simple was more likely to prove the exception than the rule – this exchange or engagement with the external world brought "an inner world . . . into being."

> The infant feels that there are parts of people and whole people inside his own body, who are alive and active, and affect him and are affected by him. Sensation, feelings, moods, affects are dominated by his relation to his inner objects.[42]

This last point drew criticism from Marjorie Brierley. She insisted on making a sharp distinction between the objective and the subjective, between "the nature of the process itself" and the "subjective significance of a given process."

> Thus, while I agree that it is imperative to recognize the continuing influence of oral experience in shaping our thinking, I do not think that intrinsic functions of the mental apparatus, such as perception and image-formation, can be adequately defined in terms of oral experience. Indeed, if we persist in equating mental functions with our subjective interpretations of them, we forfeit our claim to be scientists and revert to the primitive state of the Chinese peasant who interprets an eclipse as the sun being swallowed by a dragon. His subjective logic may be unanswerable but his explanation of the event is erroneous.[43]

On behalf of the Kleinians, Susan Isaacs responded to Brierley:

> *Now, one of the "results of the phantasy of introjection" is the process of introjection.* It is not actually bodily eating up and swallowing, but it does lead to actual, "real" alterations in the ego. These come about as a result of such a phantasy as e.g.: "I have got a good breast inside me." Or it may be "I have got a bitten-up, torturing bad breast inside me – I must kill it and get rid of it" and the like. These beliefs, which *are* figments, yet lead to real effects[,] to profound emotions, actual behaviour towards external people, profound changes in the ego, character and personality, symptoms, inhibitions and capacities. Materially, phantasies are fictions: psychically, they are realities, having real effects.[44]

Decades later Richard Wollheim echoed Isaacs's argument. In introjection, he claimed, fantasy "appears twice over":

In the first of its two appearances phantasy manifests itself in an occurrent form. A figure in the environment is perceived by the subject either as particularly loving and benign or as especially frightening and malign. . . . [I]n either case because it is perceived the way it is, the subject thereupon engages in a phantasy in which the figure . . . is depicted as being brought into the subject's body. Typically entry is effected by mouth, but sometimes through the anus. . . . In its second appearance phantasy manifests itself in a dispositional form. As a result of the incorporative phantasy the subject acquires a disposition to phantasize in a certain way. The figure whom in the incorporative phantasy he took into his body is now phantasized as engaging in a variety of activities, all of which take place within the confines of the subject.[45]

Among other Freudian texts, Heimann reminded her audience of *Totem and Taboo*; she reminded them of the "belief in the omnipotence of feelings, wishes and thought."[46] How does omnipotence of thought fit into her account? It too appears twice over. The occurrent fantasy requires omnipotence of thought as a prerequisite. The dispositional fantasy needs it to explain the effect, indeed frequently the domination, of fantasy. In this fashion the representation of one's mental processes – or prowess – turns back on itself: the belief in the omnipotence of thought is crucial to the influence that fantasy exerts.

*   *   *

The sharp disagreement – indeed animosity – between Melanie Klein and Anna Freud that reached a peak in the 1940s had a prehistory. In 1927, following the appearance of Anna Freud's *Introduction to the Technique of the Analysis of Children* (1927), the British Society held a symposium to discuss the book and then went on to publish its hard-hitting and negative appraisal.[47] In her contribution, Klein used, for illustrative purposes, the case of Erna. The 6-year-old reappeared in a number of subsequent papers, notably in the third chapter of Klein's *The Psycho-Analysis of Children* (1932). In all likelihood Erna's was the longest and most intensive child analysis that Klein conducted before moving to London in 1926: it amounted to 575 sessions over a period of 2 years and 3 months.

What had brought the girl to treatment?

Erna . . . had a number of severe symptoms She suffered from sleep-lessness, which was caused partly by anxiety (in particular by a fear of robbers and burglars) and partly by a series of obsessional activities. These consisted in lying on her face and banging her head on the pillow, in making a rocking movement, during which she sat or lay on her back, in obsessional thumb-sucking and in excessive and compulsive masturbation. And these obsessional activities which prevented her from sleeping at night, were carried on in day-time as well. This was especially the case with masturbation which she practised even in the presence of strangers. . . . She suffered from severe depressions, which she would describe by saying "There's something about life I don't like." . . . The fact that she herself felt she was ill – at the beginning of her treatment she begged me to help her – was of great assistance in analyzing her.[48]

What struck Klein was the "great aggression" in the child's games.[49]

Erna played at being a child that had dirtied itself, and I [Klein], as the mother had to scold her, whereupon she became scornful and out of defiance dirtied herself more and more. In order to annoy the mother still further she vomited up the bad food I had given her. The father was then called in by the mother, but he took the child's side. Next the mother was seized with an illness called "God has spoken to her"; then the child in turn got an illness called "mother's agitation" and died of it, and the mother was killed by the father as a punishment. The child then came to life again and was married to the father, who kept on praising it at the expense of the mother. The mother was brought to life again, too, but as a punishment was turned into a child by the father's magic wand; and now she in turn had to suffer all the humiliation and ill-treatment to which the child herself had been subjected before.

"Every educational measure," Klein surmised, "every act of nursery discipline, every unavoidable frustration," was felt by Erna "as a purely sadistic act on the part of her mother."[50]

If the mother had not actually mistreated her – and Klein found it difficult, even at the end of the treatment, to establish the connection between Erna's fantasies and reality – what had set the girl at odds with her environment? The child's own impulses, Klein argued. Early on Klein had focused on the oral-sadistic and anal-sadistic stages of libidinal development, and more specifically on their sadistic components. She came rather late to Freud's concept, first introduced in *Beyond the Pleasure Principle* (1920), of the life and death instincts. In announcing her adoption of this postulate – she did so in *The Psycho-Analysis of Children* – she aimed to secure the status of aggressive impulses as unavoidable and internal, albeit exacerbated by external frustration.

It all began, so Klein explained, with the instinctual polarity of life and death – putting the ego at immediate risk. In order to prevent the death instinct from destroying the ego, the ego deflected it outward on to the object. Now the ego's fears had a focus: its external object, though grossly distorted. Against this danger, the infant sought to defend itself by destroying the object. Sadism, of all sorts, flourished:

> The idea of an infant of from six to twelve months trying to destroy its mother by every method at the disposal of its sadistic trends – with its teeth, nails and excreta and with the whole of its body, transformed in phantasy into all kinds of dangerous weapons – presents a horrifying, not to say an unbelievable picture to our minds. . . . But the abundance, force and multiplicity of the cruel phantasies . . . displayed before our eyes in early analyses so clearly and forcibly . . . leave no room for doubt.[51]

But both deflection and attack failed: the object was not destroyed; nor did it remain external.

What happened next was that the grossly distorted object was internalized. The ego then regarded "the internalized object" as an enemy from which nothing but hostility could be expected:

> The threats of the . . . [internalized object] contain in detail the whole range of sadistic phantasies that were directed to the object, which are now turned back against the ego item by item. Thus the pressure of anxiety exerted in this early stage will correspond to the extent of sadism originally present and in quality to the variety and wealth of the accompanying sadistic phantasies.[52]

No wonder Erna felt persecuted.

Analysis made a difference: at its end, Klein reported, Erna's "phantasies of persecution were greatly reduced both in quantity and intensity."[53] From the outset, Klein – in contrast to Anna Freud – undertook "to resolve the resistances . . . in the analytic hour and to resolve in its fullness the negative transference." She had found that "if we want to make it possible for children to control their impulses better without fretting themselves in a laborious struggle with them, . . . feelings of hate . . . must be investigated down to their earliest beginnings."[54] In Erna's case the investigation remained incomplete: the girl's "sadism and anxiety could and should have been further diminished in order to prevent the possibility of an illness overtaking her at puberty or when she became a grown-up."[55] But for external reasons, the treatment had to be discontinued.

*   *   *

"The very great importance of analysing aggressive tendencies," wrote Joan Riviere in "A Contribution to the Analysis of the Negative Therapeutic Reaction" (1936), has "perhaps carried some analysts off their feet, and in some quarters" was becoming "a resistance to further analytic under-standing."[56] It was love that she feared would be given short shrift.

Klein herself took a similar line in interpreting Colette's libretto for Maurice Ravel's opera *L'Enfant et les sortilèges*. She gave this summary of the story:

> A child of six years old is sitting with his homework before him, but he is not doing any work. . . . "Don't want to do the stupid lessons," he cries in a sweet soprano. "Want to go for a walk in the park! I'd like best to eat up all the cake in the world, or pull the cat's tail or pull out all the parrot's feathers! I'd like to scold everyone! Most of all I'd like to put mama in the corner!" The door now opens. Everything on the stage is shown very large – in order to emphasize the smallness of the child – so all we see of his mother is a skirt, an apron and a hand. A finger points and a voice asks affectionately whether the child has done his work. He shuffles rebelliously on his chair and puts out his tongue at his mother. She goes away. All that we hear is the rustle of her skirts and the words: "You shall have dry bread and no sugar in your tea!" The child flies into a rage. He jumps up, drums on the door, sweeps the tea-pot and cup from the table, so that they are broken into a thousand pieces. He climbs on to the window-seat, opens the cage and tries to stab the squirrel with his pen. The squirrel escapes through the open window. The child jumps down from the window and seizes the cat. He yells and swings the tongs, pokes the fire furiously in the open grate, and with his hands and feet hurls the kettle into the room. A cloud of ashes and steam escapes. He swings the tongs like a sword and begins to tear the wallpaper. Then he opens the case of the grandfather-clock and snatches out the copper pendulum. He pours ink over the table. Exercise-books and other books fly through the air.

The child's pleasure in destruction is amply apparent: "Smashing things, tearing them up, using tongs as a sword – these represent . . . weapons of the child's primary sadism." But the sadistic attacks are only part of the story. It continues:

> The things he [the boy] has maltreated come to life. An armchair refuses to let him sit in it or have the cushions to sleep on. Table, chair, bench and sofa suddenly lift up their arms and cry: "Away with the dirty little creature!" The clock has a dreadful stomach-ache and begins to strike the hours like mad. The tea-pot leans over the cup, and they begin to talk in Chinese. Everything undergoes a terrifying change. The child falls back against the wall and shudders with fear and desolation. The stove spits out a shower of sparks at him. He hides behind the furniture. The shreds of the torn wallpaper begin to sway and stand up,

showing shepherdesses and sheep. The shepherd's pipe sounds a
heartbreaking lament; the rent in the paper . . . has become a rent in the
fabric of the world! But the doleful tale dies away. From under the
cover of a book . . . there . . . emerges a little red man. . . . He holds a
ruler and clatters about with little dancing steps. He is the spirit of
mathematics, and begins to put the child through an examination:
millimetre, centimetre, barometer, trillion – eight and eight are forty.
Three times nine is twice six. The child falls down in a faint!

Half suffocated he takes refuge in the park round the house. . . .
[T]here again the air is full of terror, insects, frogs (lamenting in muted
thirds), a wounded tree-trunk, which oozes resin in long-drawn-out
bass notes, dragon-flies and oleander-flies all attack the newcomer.
Owl, cats and squirrels come along in hosts. The dispute as to who is to
bite the child becomes a hand-to-hand fight. A squirrel which has been
bitten falls to the ground screaming beside him. He instinctively takes
off his scarf and binds up the little creature's paw. There is great
amazement amongst the animals, who gather together hesitatingly in
the background. The child has whispered: "Mama!" He is restored to
the human world of helping, "being good." "That's a good child, a
very well-behaved child," sing the animals very seriously in a soft
march – the finale of the piece – as they leave the stage.

"When the boy feels pity for the wounded squirrel and comes to its aid,"
Klein noted, "the hostile world changes into a friendly one." She added:
"The child has learnt to love and believes in love."[57]

By the 1940s, Klein was ready to put love and hate on an equal footing.
(That had not always been the case. Klein's earlier work suggested a certain
asymmetry: bad objects derived from a child's sadism; good objects from
the external world; bad objects differed fundamentally from the real
objects; good objects more closely approximated actual mothers who had
been on hand in early infancy.) Her adoption of the death instinct – and its
companion, the life instinct – provided a theoretical rationale:

> The activity of the death instinct deflected outwards, as well as its
> working within, cannot be considered apart from the simultaneous
> activity of the life instinct. Side by side with the deflection of the death
> instinct outwards, the life instinct . . . attaches to the external object,
> the gratifying (good) breast, which becomes the external representative
> of the life instinct. The introjection of this good object reinforces the
> power of the life instinct within. . . . The good internalized breast and
> the bad devouring breast . . . are the representatives within the ego of
> the struggle between the life and death instincts.[58]

Elsewhere Klein moved from Eros and Thanatos, from the speculative and
quasi-biological, to the empirical and psychological:

> Whether elements . . . of love are present even in the earliest relation of the infant to the mother's breast remains a theoretical problem to be further elucidated; but the fact that love in some sense is discernible within the earliest stages has been acknowledged by a number of observers approaching the study of the infant from various theoretical angles.[59]

A capacity for love as well as a capacity for hate – Klein thought of them both as innate[60] – constituted conceptual bedrock.

Bedrock for what? For bringing the conflict between love and hate – the conflict due to ambivalence – front and center. This had also been a dominant concern in Freud's thought. But for Freud ambivalence owed its centrality not to his belated formulation of the life and death instincts, nor to innate capacities for loving and hating; it owed its centrality to Oedipus, the nuclear complex of the neuroses. Klein, in effect, extricated ambivalence from that complex and embedded it instead in the depressive position.

*   *   *

By the time of the Controversial Discussions, Klein had already published her two path-breaking papers on the depressive position: "A Contribution to the Psychogenesis of Manic-Depressive States" (1935) and "Mourning and its Relation to Manic-Depressive States" (1940). In them she sought to describe the building up of an internal world and to chart the vicissitudes of object relations within it.

Why "position"? Klein needed a term to designate particular groupings of anxieties, defenses, and internal object relationships. She wanted to get away from the notion of stages or phases of development, which her work with children had suggested to her were overlapping rather than clear cut. She wanted to convey, with her idea of positions, that the groupings so labeled were not rigid and inflexible; fluctuations were possible, indeed usual – and not just in the child.[61]

Recall the presence of good and bad objects. Initially such objects were not whole objects; they were part objects, and the mother's breast was the prototype. It was a development of the highest importance when an infant took the step from "a partial object-relation to the relation with a complete object."[62] (In the Controversial Discussions Klein toned down the significance of this step and simply assumed "that the mother as a whole object however vague in outline exists from the beginning in the infant's mind.")[63] Wholeness – whenever it came to be recognized – heightened the likelihood that the ego would "identify itself more fully with 'good objects.'" This last phrase is obscure: "identify" gives trouble. Klein did not mean that the "ego" – infant would have been more appropriate here – tried to be like its good external object. Rather she meant that the infant became dependent upon it, and upon its internalized counterpart, with a new force: "From now on preservation of the good object is regarded as synonymous with the survival of the ego."[64]

Thus the infant comes to the anxieties that marked the depressive position. (The word "depressive" may also give trouble. As Donald W. Winnicott noted, the term "seems to imply that infants . . . pass through a stage of depression or mood illness." But Klein was not, in fact, describing infants who are "depersonalized and hopeless about external contacts"; such infants lack the prerequisite, the relationship to a whole good object, for entering the depressive position.)[65] The infant felt "constantly menaced" in his "possession of internalized good objects"; he was "full of anxiety lest such objects should die." And these good objects were threatened from all sides. "It is not only the vehemence of the subject's uncontrollable hatred but that of his love too which imperils the object. For at this stage of his development loving an object and devouring it are very closely connected." A little child who believed, when his mother disappeared, that he had "eaten her up and destroyed her (whether from motives of love or of hate) is tormented by anxiety."[66] In short, there seemed to be no way for the child to avoid inflicting damage on his good object.

No wonder, then, that anxiety alone did not dominate the picture; guilt and remorse were its constant companions.

> Full identification with the object based on the libidinal attachment, first to the breast, then to the whole person, goes hand in hand with anxiety for it (of its disintegration), with guilt and remorse, with a sense of responsibility for preserving it intact against persecutors . . ., and with sadness relating to expectations of the impending loss of it.[67]

Reparation gone awry

Recall Klein's commentary on *L'Enfant et les sortilèges*; recall the boy's pity for the wounded squirrel and his effort to tend the small creature. The boy had certainly exhibited "primitive tendencies"; now he was trying "to make good and to atone" for the damage he had done.[68] And all at once the hostile world changed into a friendly one.

When Klein formulated the concept of the depressive position, reparation, which she had spotted in Colette's libretto, moved to the fore.

> We find them [tendencies to make reparation] at work in the first play activities and at the basis of the child's satisfaction in his achievements, even those of the most simple kind for example, in putting one brick on top of another, or making a brick stand upright after it had been knocked down – all this is partly derived from the unconscious phantasy of making some kind of restoration to some person or several persons whom he has injured in phantasy.[69]

Reparation, according to Klein, was concerned primarily with the state of the internal world; yet it was usually expressed in action toward objects in the external world, toward objects which represented the damaged internal object. Reparation, and the belief in its possibility, was thus a force both for securing the internal world and for constructive action in the external one.

Riviere, in her paper on the negative therapeutic reaction, shifted the focus from children to patients – more particularly to the patient who failed to benefit from treatment. For the latter, reparation figured not as an ordinary developmental step but as a monumental task that threatened to overwhelm him. She sketched his great fear:

> [I]f he were cured by analysis, faithfully and truly, and made at last able to compass the reparation needed by all those he loved and injured, . . . the magnitude of the task would then absorb his whole self with every atom of all its resources, his whole physical and mental powers as long as he lives, every breath, every heartbeat, drop of blood, every thought, every moment of time, every possession, all money, every vestige of any capacity he has – an extremity of slavery and self-immolation which passes conscious understanding. This is what cure means to him from his unconscious depressive standpoint, and his uncured *status quo* in an unending analysis is clearly preferable to such a conception of cure – however grandiose and magnificent . . . its appeal may be.[70]

And it was this sort of fear that Riviere discerned lurking in Ibsen's *The Master Builder*.[71]

*   *   *

Solness – the master builder – has reached the peak of success in his profession and has seemingly attained everything or almost everything that life has to offer. But "he is revealed as moody and unreasonable, overtly or tacitly harsh to all, . . . preyed upon by anxiety" – and haunted by the past:

> Twelve years before, soon after his marriage, the gloomy old family mansion inherited by his wife from her parents, in which he and she lived, was burnt to the ground, and the insurance compensation obtained from it enabled him to extend his business very substantially. But his advantage was accompanied by a tragedy; his young wife had given birth to twin sons just before the fire, and the shock and effects of the catastrophic destruction of her home and her removal with the babies during the fire had disastrous consequences for her and them. She lost her milk; the babies died; and she was thrown into a depression from which she will never recover. We see her now as a withdrawn . . . figure, almost without contacts, either sunk in melancholy, self-reproaches

and regrets or mechanically occupied with her "duty" in small house-
hold tasks.[72]

The major action of the play takes place between the master builder and
a young girl – Hilda – who suddenly knocks on the door and enters the
scene. Who is this fantastic and headstrong creature?

> Ten years before Solness had built a church with a high tower . . . in
> Hilda's native town, and she as a child of eleven had watched the
> celebrations at its completion, when he had climbed to its pinnacle by
> the scaffolding and had hung a wreath there. The little girl was intoxi-
> cated by the excitement of the incident, cheered and sang among the
> loudest, afterwards waylaid him in her father's house, evoked such a
> response from him that he kissed her ardently, promised her to come
> back . . . for her in ten years' time, make her a Princess and give her a
> kingdom. It is ten years to the day when she walks upon the stage and
> says she has come for her kingdom![73]

Can she bend him to her will? A new tower on a new house is to be finished
that very evening. Hilda longs to see Solness repeat his feat, to see him with
wreath in hand, high, high up on a tower. She insists that he must climb it
and again set a wreath on the height. He yields to her spell and mounts to
the top; but as he waves to her and she to him, he falls. So ends his attempt
to escape to a castle in the air.

Escape from what? Early in the play Solness speaks of his "huge,
immeasurable debt" to his wife. Later in an attempt to explain his
indebtedness, he tells Hilda at length about the fire.

SOLNESS   (*speaking low with inward emotion*): Mark what I say to you,
            Hilda. All that I have succeeded in doing, building, creating – all
            the beauty, security, cheerful comfort – ay, and magnificence too
            – (*Clenches his hands.*) Oh, is it not terrible to think of –!
HILDA: What is so terrible?
SOLNESS: That all I have to make up for, to pay for – not in money, but in
            human happiness. And not with my own happiness only, but with
            other people's too. Yes, yes, do you see that, Hilda? That is the
            price which my position as an artist has cost me – and others.
            And every single day I have to look on while the price is paid for
            me anew. Over again, and over again – and over again for ever!
HILDA: (*rises and looks steadily at him*): Now I can see that you are
            thinking of – of her.
SOLNESS: Yes, mainly of Aline [Mrs. Solness]. For Aline – she, too, had her
            vocation in life, just as much as I had mine. (*His voice quivers.*)
            But her vocation had to be stunted, and crushed, and shattered –

in order that mine might force its way to – to a sort of great victory. For you must know that Aline – she, too, had a talent for building.

HILDA: She! For building?

SOLNESS: (*shakes his head*): Not houses and towers, and spires – not such things as I work away at –

HILDA: Well, but what then?

SOLNESS: (*softly with emotion*): For building up the souls of little children, Hilda. For building up children's souls in perfect balance, and in noble and beautiful forms. For enabling them to soar up into erect and full-grown human souls. That was Aline's talent. And there it all lies now – unused and unusable for ever. . . . Just like the ruins left by a fire. . . .

HILDA: Well, but in any case it is not your fault. . . .

SOLNESS: Yes. Suppose the fault was mine – in a certain sense.

HILDA: Your fault! The fire! . . .

SOLNESS: (*with a quiet, chuckling laugh*): Just sit down again, Hilda, and I'll tell you something funny.

HILDA: (*sits down; with intent interest*): Well?

SOLNESS: It sounds such a ludicrous little thing; for, you see, the whole story turns upon nothing but a crack in a chimney.

HILDA: No more than that?

SOLNESS: No, not to begin with. (*He moves a chair nearer to* HILDA *and sits down.*)

HILDA: (*impatiently, taps her knee*): Well, now for the crack in the chimney!

SOLNESS: I had noticed the split in the flue long, long, before the fire. Every time I went up into the attic, I looked to see if it was still there.

HILDA: And it was?

SOLNESS: Yes, for no one else knew about it.

HILDA: And you said nothing?

SOLNESS: Nothing.

HILDA: And did not think of repairing the flue either?

SOLNESS: Oh yes, I thought about it – but never got any further. Every time I intended to set to work, it seemed just as if a hand held me back. Not to-day, I thought – to-morrow; and nothing came of it.

HILDA: But why did you keep putting it off like that?

SOLNESS: Because I was revolving something in my mind. (*Slowly, and in a low voice.*) Through that little black crack in the chimney, I might, perhaps force my way upwards – as a builder.

HILDA: (*looking straight in front of her*): That must have been thrilling.

SOLNESS: Almost irresistible – quite irresistible. For all that time it appeared to me a perfectly simple and straight-forward matter. I would have had it happen in the winter-time – a little before

	midday. I was to be out driving Aline in the sleigh. . . . And as we drove home, we were to see the smoke.
HILDA:	Only the smoke?
SOLNESS:	The smoke first. But when we came up to the garden gate, the whole of the old timber-box was to be a rolling mass of flames. – That is how I wanted it to be, you see.
HILDA:	Oh why, why could it not have happened so!
SOLNESS:	You may well say that, Hilda.
HILDA:	Well, but now listen, Mr. Solness. Are you perfectly certain that the fire was caused by that little crack in the chimney?
SOLNESS:	No, on the contrary – I am perfectly certain that the crack in the chimney had nothing whatever to do with the fire.
HILDA:	What?
SOLNESS:	It was been clearly ascertained that the fire broke out in a clothes-cupboard – in a totally different part of the house.
HILDA:	Then what is all this nonsense you are talking about the crack in the chimney?[74]

Hilda responds to Solness's disquisition with a diagnosis: he suffers from a "sickly conscience," by which she means, "too delicately built . . . hasn't strength to take a grip of things – to lift and bear what is heavy."[75] Riviere offered a diagnosis of her own: Hilda personified the "manic defence"; there could be no "plainer representation" of it than in this character.[76] And it is along a manic path that Hilda leads Solness.

In *Group Psychology* Freud had mentioned the abrogation of a domineering ego ideal and the magnificent – manic – festival for the ego that followed. Riviere, in her paper on the negative therapeutic reaction, extended his thought: she wrote of a "manic attitude" or "manic defence." This was no momentary rebellion; this was a "highly organized system of defence against a more or less unconscious depressive condition in the patient."

> The essential feature of the manic attitude is omnipotence and the *omnipotent denial of psychical reality*, which of course leads to a distorted and defective sense of external reality. . . . The *denial* relates especially to the ego's object-relations and its *dependence on its objects*, as a result of which *contempt* and depreciation of the value of its objects is a marked feature, together with attempts at inordinate and tyrannical *control and mastery of its objects*.

And in Riviere's view there was "all the difference in the world between what may be called single isolated interpretations, however correct and however frequent they may be, and the understanding and interpretation of such detailed instances as part of a general *organized system of defence* . . ., with all its links and ramifications spreading far and wide in the symptom-picture, in the formation of character and in the behaviour patterns of the patient."[77]

Solness's manic posture is literally untenable and proves fatal. Offstage manic defenses may not produce so dramatic a reversal of fortune; but, all the same, as Klein pointed out in her paper on mourning, they are likely to spoil attempts at reparation, to spoil, for example, the boy's gesture toward the wounded squirrel, a gesture that turned a hostile world into a friendly one:

> The desire to control the object, the sadistic gratification of . . . getting the better of it, the *triumph* over it, may enter so strongly into the act of reparation (carried out by thoughts, activities or sublimations) that the "benign" circle started by this act becomes broken. The objects which were to be restored change again into persecutors. . . . The reparation which was in progress is . . . disturbed and even nullified – according to the extent to which these mechanisms are activated. As a result of the failure of the act of reparation, the ego has to resort again and again to . . . manic defences.[78]

*   *   *

Looking back over the material covered in this chapter, I want to highlight the vicissitudes that guilt has undergone. In *Group Psychology* Freud gave it a theoretical formulation: he construed guilt "as an expression of the tension between the ego and the ego ideal."[79] He also raised the possibility of a manic escape from that tension. But he did not appreciate that identification with an idealized figure – on which he thought group life rested – had something of the manic about it, that like a manic defensive system, it entailed the denial of psychical reality.

Klein built on the analysis of the ego that Freud had adumbrated in *Group Psychology* and at the same time retained and developed the themes he had broached in *Totem and Taboo*. She took off from Freud's discussion of introjection and projection to conceptualize a world of internal objects – "a complex object-world, which is felt by the individual, in deep layers of the unconscious, to be concretely inside himself."

> This inner world consists of innumerable objects taken into the ego, corresponding . . . to the multitude of varying aspects, good and bad, in which the parents (and other people), appeared to the child's unconscious mind throughout various stages of his development. . . . In addition, all these objects are . . . in an infinitely complex relation both with each other and with the self.[80]

The depressive position, then, constituted an account of those complex relations – of the self's fear for its good objects, of its guilt about destructive impulses toward them, of its desire to repair the damage inflicted on them, and of its grief over failing to do so.

Thus ambivalence, largely absent from *Group Psychology*, took center stage in Klein's thinking. Having anchored it in Freud's dual instinct theory, she argued that the conflicting feelings gave rise to a particular type of anxiety – depressive anxiety. "[I]s guilt," she asked, "an element in depressive anxiety? Are they both aspects of the same process, or is one the result or a manifestation of the other?" She ventured no "definite answer";[81] her followers were less tentative. Among them there was a general consensus that once an individual realized "that the object he loves is also the object against whom he rages and feels anger," he feels guilty – "guilt is fatally inevitable."[82]

And finally, omnipotence of thought, also missing from *Group Psychology*, proved crucial to Klein's theorizing. She first leaned on this notion in describing the construction of an inner world. The fantasy of incorporation, for example, presupposes a belief in the omnipotence of thought, and the same belief contributes mightily to the influence the incorporated or introjected objects wield. Subsequently, she and Riviere discerned a "special development and application" of omnipotence in "the manic defence against depressive anxieties."[83] Here was the beginning of an explanation of how those anxieties were warded off and/or defended against.

Chapter 3

Omnipotence holding sway

In *Civilization and Its Discontents* (1930), Freud reminded his readers once again of the claims he had made in *Totem and Taboo*. In that earlier work, he wrote, he had "tried to show how the way led from . . . [the primitive] family to the succeeding stage of communal life in the form of bands of brothers."

> In overpowering their father, the sons had made the discovery that a combination can be stronger than a single individual. The totemic culture is based on the restrictions which the sons had to impose on one another in order to keep this new state of affairs in being. The taboo-observances were the first . . . "law."

In *Civilization and Its Discontents* Freud elaborated on those restrictions. At the same time he turned his full attention to guilt and took care to justify this preoccupation:

> I suspect that the reader has the impression that our discussions on the sense of guilt disrupt the framework of this essay: that they take up too much space, so that the rest of the subject-matter . . . is pushed to one side. This may have spoilt the structure of my paper; but it corresponds faithfully to my intention to represent the sense of guilt as the most important problem in the development of civilization and to show that the price we pay for our advance in civilization is a loss of happiness through a heightening of the sense of guilt.[1]

Here was a marked shift from *Group Psychology and the Analysis of the Ego* (1921). In *Civilization and Its Discontents* guilt not only figured prominently; it had turned persecutory as well. Beyond that, Freud argued that this ferocity did not reflect the harshness with which a child's parents had behaved toward him. Sándor Ferenczi, for one, objected: "[W]ould it not be more correct to hold fast to the individually acquired (i.e. traumatic) nature, that is to say, origin, of conscience . . . , and to maintain that the all too strict conscience . . . is the result of a *relatively too strict* treatment – i.e., too strict in relation to the individually varied need for love." He objected to the way Freud, on this question, had accepted "the view of Melanie Klein."[2]

In 1930, when he acknowledged his debt to Klein, Freud was nearing the end of his career; Klein was just getting into full swing. No wonder, then, that it was she who worked out the notion of conscience as persecutory, a notion that might be regarded as the product of an unusual – and distant – collaboration between the two of them. Initially Klein outlined a paranoid position; only after the Second World War did she add schizoid phenomena to the mix and arrive at her formulation of a paranoid-schizoid position. Throughout these years she never lost interest in guilt, though keeping it in her sights proved difficult. So elusive could it be that many psychoanalysts would have sworn that the patient did not feel it, perhaps never had, and indeed might be judged incapable of harboring such sentiments.

This was a line that Klein's students refused to take. Successive generations of her followers assumed – and it proved to be a fruitful assumption – that it was up to the psychoanalyst to figure out how complex and multi-layered defenses shielded the patient from a sense of guilt that had become interlaced with persecution. Influenced also by Joan Riviere, Hanna Segal and John Steiner, among others, expanded and elaborated on the manic defense and its "special development . . . of omnipotence."[3]

Civilization and Its Discontents

In his 1930 text Freud told the following tale. It was a tale in which external authority figured as crucial:

> To begin with, if we ask how a person comes to have a sense of guilt, we arrive at an answer which cannot be disputed: a person feels guilty (devout people would say "sinful") when he has done something which he knows to be "bad." But then we notice how little this answer tells us. . . . How is this judgement [of what is bad] arrived at? . . . What is bad is often not at all what is injurious or dangerous to the ego; on the contrary, it may be something which is desirable and enjoyable. . . . Here, therefore, there is an extraneous influence at work, and it is this that decides what is to be called good or bad.

Another question immediately posed itself: why was the external authority accepted as personally binding?

> Such a motive is easily discovered in . . . [a person's] helplessness and his dependence on other people, and it can best be designated as fear of loss of love. If he loses the love of another person on whom he is

dependent, he also ceases to be protected from a variety of dangers. . . .
At the beginning, therefore, what is bad is whatever causes one to be
threatened with loss of love.

Beyond that, a "great change" took place when the authority – principally
the father – was "internalized through the establishment of a super-ego. At
this point . . . the distinction . . . between doing something bad and wishing
to do it" disappeared entirely, since nothing could "be hidden from the
super-ego, not even thoughts." In this fashion Freud arrived at "two origins
of the sense of guilt: one arising from the fear of an authority, and the other,
later on, arising from fear of the super-ego." Actually, he claimed, only with
the establishment of the superego should "we . . . speak of conscience or a
sense of guilt."[4]

With a paternal figure hovering over the scene, Freud moved on – along
an associative path – to *Totem and Taboo*. He reminded the reader of the
argument he had advanced in that earlier work, that the sense of guilt went
"back to the killing of the primal father."

Are we to assume that . . . a conscience and a sense of guilt were not, as
we have presupposed, in existence before the deed? If not, where, in this
case, did remorse come from? . . . This remorse was the result of the
primordial ambivalence of feeling toward the father. His sons hated
him, but they loved him, too. After their hatred had been satisfied by
their act of aggression, their love came to the fore in their remorse for
the deed. It set up the super-ego by identification with the father; it
gave the agency the father's power, as though as a punishment for the
deed of aggression they had carried out against him, and it created the
restrictions which were intended to prevent a repetition of the deed.
And since the inclination to aggressiveness against the father was
repeated in the following generations, the sense of guilt, too, persisted.
. . . Whether one has killed one's father or has abstained from doing so
is not really the decisive thing. One is bound to feel guilty in either case,
for the sense of guilt is an expression of the conflict due to ambivalence,
of the eternal struggle between Eros and the instinct of destruction
or death.

Freud quickly appreciated that he had landed in an inconsistency: on the
one hand, he insisted that one "ought not to speak of conscience until a
super-ego is demonstrably present";[5] on the other, he claimed that the
ambivalence, so characteristic of relations of children to their parents,
created in the children genuine moral sensibilities even before a conscience
or superego was in place.[6]

*   *   *

In the late 1920s Klein too was struggling with the notion of the superego and the origins of guilt. As a first step she stressed the ways in which oedipal dramas overlapped and coincided with libidinal trends. (Where Freud retained two separate developmental lines, object love and libido, whose convergence at a fairly late date produced the Oedipus complex, she assumed that so clear a distinction was more misleading than helpful.) As a second step she argued that the superego took shape in tandem with the Oedipus complex – not after its demolition. (Still more, rather than taking positive and negative elements and arranging them in a limited number of fixed patterns, Klein was intent on transforming the Oedipus complex into a fluctuating configuration.) Both were set in motion when the oral-sadistic and anal-sadistic stages were "fully at work"; both oedipal objects and superego were then endowed with the intense sadism belonging to those stages. Thus it had been with 4-year-old Gerald:

> One of his anxiety-objects we ascertained during the analysis was a beast . . . , but in reality was a man. This beast, which made big noises in the next room, was the father from whom the noises emanated in the adjoining bedroom. The desire of Gerald to penetrate there, to blind the father, to castrate and to kill him caused a dread that he would be treated in the same way by the beast.[7]

Yet, the little boy, who "suffered from the pressure of a castrating and cannibalistic super-ego" had "certainly not only this one super-ego":

> I discovered in him identifications which corresponded more closely to his real parents, though not by any means identical with them. These figures, who appeared good and helpful and ready to forgive, he called his "fairy papa and mamma," and when his attitude towards me was positive, he allowed me in the analysis to play the part of the "fairy mamma" to whom everything could be confessed. At other times . . . I played the part of the wicked mamma from whom everything evil that he phantasied was anticipated. . . . A whole series of [the] most varied identifications, which were in opposition to one another, originated in widely different strata and periods and differed fundamentally from the real objects, had in this child resulted in a super-ego which actually gave the impression of being normal and well-developed.[8]

Klein herself had no vested interest in regarding the superego as a unitary structure. For her (as well as for Freud) the superego had at least two recognizably different tasks: as the agent of prohibition and punishment and as "the advocate of a striving toward perfection" or the "ideal,"[9] Two sets of parental images were playing two different roles: parents as terrifying figures who were hated and feared and parents as ideal figures.

Recall that in Klein's view introjection and projection began with birth itself.

> [These] processes . . . lead to the institution inside ourselves of loved and hated objects, who are felt to be "good" and "bad," and who are interrelated with each other and with the self. . . . This assembly of internalized objects becomes organized, together with the organization of the ego, and in the higher strata of the mind it becomes discernible as the super-ego. Thus, the phenomenon which was recognized by Freud, broadly speaking, as the voices and the influence of the actual parents established in the ego, is according to my findings, a complex object-world.[10]

Following this line of argument, a half-decade later, Klein arrived at the concept of the depressive position and the centrality of ambivalence in giving rise to moral sentiments – too late for Freud to make use of it.

*   *   *

To turn to the harshness of the superego – intellectual property shared by Freud and Klein alike. Freud gave the following summary of his argument:

> Originally, renunciation of instinct was the result of fear of an external authority: one renounced one's satisfactions in order not to lose its love. If one carried out this renunciation, one is, as it were, quits with the authority and no sense of guilt should remain. But with fear of the super-ego the case is different. Here instinctual renunciation is not enough, for the wish persists and cannot be concealed from the super-ego. Thus, in spite of the renunciation that has been made, a sense of guilt comes about. . . . Instinctual renunciation now no longer has a completely liberating effect; virtuous continence is no longer rewarded with the assurance of love. A threatened external unhappiness – loss of love and punishment on the part of the external authority – has been exchanged for a permanent internal unhappiness, for the tension of the sense of guilt.[11]

He himself was dissatisfied: he had not adequately explained the superego's cruel treatment of the ego.

Freud offered two hypotheses. According to the first, the "severity of the super-ego . . . represents one's own aggressiveness. . . . In the beginning conscience arises through the suppression of an aggressive impulse, and . . . it is subsequently reinforced by fresh suppressions of the same kind." In sum, the superego "enters into possession of all the aggressiveness which the child would have liked to exercise" against the original external authority. According to the second hypothesis, "the aggressiveness of conscience keeps up with the aggressiveness of the authority." It is not difficult, he added, "to convince oneself that severity of upbringing does . . . exert a strong influence on the formation of the child's super-ego." In other words, the severity of one's conscience is a continuation of the harsh treatment one received from those who exercised authority over one in one's childhood.[12]

Freud refused to choose between the two suppositions. Indeed he regarded both as justified. On the one hand, he claimed that "experience shows . . . that the severity of the super-ego which a child develops in no way corresponds to the severity of the treatment which he has himself met with."[13] (Here Freud's footnote read: "As has rightly been emphasized by Melanie Klein and other English writers.")[14] "The severity of the former," he added, "seems to be independent of the latter." Then he backtracked. On the other hand, he concluded "it would be wrong to exaggerate this independence. . . . [I]nnate constitutional factors and influences from the real environment act in combination."[15] And over the course of time Klein herself became more broad-minded; she became more willing to consider that environment as well as constitution had a part to play.

Freud and Klein, then, did not differ over the ferocity of the superego – though her language, her descriptions of a small child being "dominated by the fear of . . . unimaginable cruel attacks, both from its real objects and its super-ego" – was far more dramatic than his.[16] But here he effectively came to a halt; in contrast she pressed on. By 1930 Freud had his major discoveries behind him – not least the superego and unconscious feelings of guilt; Klein had several productive decades ahead of her – including the exploration of persecutory fears at their most intense.

To the paranoid-schizoid position

At the meeting of the British Psycho-Analytical Society held on December 17, 1943, Paula Heimann and Susan Isaacs circulated their paper – the third in the Controversial Discussions – entitled "Regression." Their aim – and Klein's as well – was to broaden a concept which Freud had introduced in connection with stages of libidinal development. Regression had been understood as a retreat to an earlier point, say, as with obsessional neurotics to the anal-sadistic stage. Now Heimann and Isaacs insisted that "internal objects and the superego" played an essential part in "the regressive process."[17] And they cited Freud's *Inhibitions, Symptoms and Anxiety* (1926) to buttress their claim: in obsessional neurotics along with "a regressive degradation of the libido," the superego became "exceptionally severe and unkind."[18] The movement, then, of interest to Klein and her followers was not backward to a fixation point but rather a movement between overlapping positions, the depressive and the paranoid.

In her paper "A Contribution to the Psychogenesis of Manic-Depressive States" (1935), to illustrate that to-and-fro, Klein cited the case of patient X, who, as a child, had been told that he had tapeworms and had "connected the tapeworms . . . with his greediness."

> In his analysis he had phantasies that a tapeworm was eating its way through his body and a strong anxiety of cancer came to the fore. The patient, who suffered from hypochondriacal and paranoid anxieties, was very suspicious of me, and, among other things, suspected me of being allied with people who were hostile to him. At this time he dreamt that a detective was arresting a hostile and persecuting person and putting this person in prison. But then the detective proved unreliable and became the accomplice of the enemy. The detective stood for myself. . . . The prison in which the enemy was kept was his own inside. . . . It became clear that the dangerous tapeworm (one of his associations was that the tapeworm was bisexual) represented the two parents in a hostile alliance . . . against him. . . .
>
> [W]hen the tapeworm-phantasies were being analysed the patient developed diarrhoea which – as X wrongly thought – was mixed with blood. This frightened him very much; he felt it as a confirmation of dangerous processes going on inside him. This feeling was founded on phantasies in which he attacked his bad united parents in his inside with poisonous excreta. . . . In his early childhood he had in phantasy attacked his real parents with poisonous excreta and actually disturbed them in intercourse by defaecating. . . . Along with these attacks on his real parents his whole warfare became internalized and threatened his ego with destruction. I may mention that this patient remembered during his analysis that at about ten years of age he had definitely felt that he had a little man inside his stomach who controlled him and gave him orders, which he, the patient, had to execute, although they were always perverse and wrong (he had had similar feelings about his real father's requests).
>
> When the analysis progressed and distrust in me had diminished, the patient became very much concerned with me. X had always worried about his mother's health; but he had not been able to develop real love towards her, though he did his best to please her. Now, together with the concern for me, strong feelings of love and gratitude came to the fore, together with feelings of unworthiness, sorrow and depression. . . . At the same time the feelings and phantasies connected with his hypo-chondriacal pains changed. For instance, the patient felt anxiety that the cancer would make its way through the lining of his stomach; but now it appeared that while he feared for his stomach, he really wanted to protect "me" inside him – actually the internalized mother – who he felt was being attacked by the father's penis and his own id (the

cancer). . . . It became clear now that the cancer which he made
responsible for the death of his loved object, as well as for his own, and
which stood for the bad father's penis, was even more felt to be his own
sadism, especially his greed.

Klein summed up: "While the paranoid anxiety predominated and the
anxiety of his bad united objects prevailed, X felt only hypochondriacal
anxieties for his own body. When depression and sorrow had set in, the
love and the concern for the good object came to the fore and the anxiety
contents . . . altered."[19]

Beyond the shift from the paranoid to the depressive – and it was in this
paper that Klein referred to them as positions – she discerned a counter-
point: "*paranoid fears and suspicions were reinforced as a defence against the
depressive position.*"[20] Elsewhere she provided more detail:

> [D]uring a particular session a patient may suffer from strong feelings
> of guilt and despair about his incapacity to restore the damage he feels
> he has caused. Then a complete change occurs: the patient suddenly
> brings up material of a persecutory kind. The analyst and analysis are
> accused of doing nothing but harm, grievances which lead back to early
> frustrations are voiced. . . . [P]ersecutory anxiety has become dominant,
> the feeling of guilt has receded, and with it the love for the object seems
> to have disappeared. In this altered emotional situation, the object has
> turned bad, cannot be loved, and therefore destructive impulses
> towards it seem justified. This means that persecutory anxiety and
> defences *have been reinforced* in order to escape from the overwhelming
> burden of guilt and despair.[21]

*   *   *

The oscillation between depressive and persecutory feelings, the splitting of
objects between good and bad, the conflict between love and hate – all this
theoretical equipment was on display in Klein's treatment of 10-year-old
Richard. From the outset both he and she knew that the analysis would
have to be brief – 93 sessions in all as it turned out. Its brevity, imposed by
wartime circumstances – the year was 1941 – made possible the daily
account Klein wanted to put together. Hence she determined to keep a
record that would subsequently allow her to write up the case. (Klein was
still going through the proofs and index of *Narrative of a Child Analysis* at
the time of her death in 1960.) Her detailed notes were not verbatim
reports; she agreed with Freud, who had warned that note taking during a
session diverted "the analyst's attention from the course of the analysis."[22]
So she took her extensive notes after the session; as a result she could not be
absolutely "sure of the sequence," nor could she "quote literally the
patient's associations" or her own interpretations.[23]

The short span of the analysis was unusual; the same was true of the setting. At the time, Klein was staying in Pitlochry, a Scottish village, and was renting a playroom, since her lodgings were unsuitable for child patients. The playroom, "though . . . large . . . with two doors and an adjoining kitchen and lavatory," had drawbacks. It was used by Girl Guides, and Klein had to leave in place a number of their books, pictures, and maps. "The absence of a waiting room and the fact that there was nobody to answer the door" meant that Klein had to fetch the key, unlock the room, and lock it up again, before and after each session. Thus some conversation with Richard outside the playroom was unavoidable. The surroundings were strange to Richard as well. For the duration of the war, he and his family had settled in a locale not too far from Pitlochry. During the week, Richard and his mother stayed in a hotel in that village. These arrangements imposed a strain on the boy; and it was compounded first by a brief illness of his mother's and then by a heart attack his father suffered. Despite the obstacles due to time and place, Klein believed that she had reached the troubled child and enabled him "to become conscious of some of his anxieties and defences" – though an "adequate working-through was not possible."[24]

What was the matter with Richard? Klein gave no precise answer in terms of the then-current notions of psychopathology. But she did furnish a description of this severely incapacitated boy. Since about the age of 4 or 5, Richard had suffered from a "progressive inhibition of his faculties and interests," accompanied by hypochondriacal symptoms and depressed moods. By the age of 8 he had become so frightened of other children that he had to stop attending school. His fears gradually increased to the point where he was scarcely able to go out by himself. The war, quite naturally, exacerbated his difficulties.[25] The fact that he managed to cope with his stressful living arrangements suggested his commitment to his analytic treatment.

Although Richard was terrified of children, he could get on with adults, particularly with women. "He tried to impress them with his conversational gifts and to ingratiate himself in a rather precocious way." Certainly his behavior differed from what Klein regarded as typical of the latency period: he lacked that "general attitude of reserve and distrust" which made children his age "deeply averse to anything" that savored of "search and interrogation."[26] One might be tempted to dismiss his ease with Klein as part of his symptomatology were it not for the depth of the communications he was able to make. "He could verbalize his feelings, memories, and anxieties to her, and was also very open in his disagreements as well as agreements."[27] Richard, desperate for help, and Klein, eager to provide it, lost no time in setting down to work.

Here is the first session. (Klein, under the pressure of time, seems to be in a great hurry.) Richard readily proceeded to "talk about his worries." He ticked off his fear of going out in the street, his school phobia, and his uneasiness about the war. The war was his dominant concern: he hoped that Hitler would be beaten; he spoke of the cruel treatment of conquered countries, Austria among them; he gave a dramatic account of how the family cook had been frightened when a bomb had fallen near their former house. "After that he tried to remember whether he had any worries he had not yet mentioned. Oh yes, he often wondered what he was like inside and what other people's insides were like." Klein interposed with a question – an unusual move for her to have made: she asked "whether he also worried about his mother sometimes." This query opened up a new vein. Richard talked about his night terrors and how these terrors centered on his mother: "In the evenings he often feared that a nasty man – a kind of tramp – would come and kidnap Mummy during the night." At this point Klein began to interpret:

> *Mrs. K.* suggested that the tramp who would hurt Mummy at night seemed to him very much like Hitler who frightened Cook in the air-raid and ill-treated the Austrians. Richard knew that Mrs. K. was Austrian, and so she too would be ill-treated. At night he might have been afraid when his parents went to bed something could happen between their genitals that would injure Mummy.

Richard did not fully understand. He had not learned the word "genital"; he had no conception of sexual intercourse; he had only vague notions about eggs, fluids, babies, and mothers' insides. Klein explained the term and continued:

> *Mrs. K.* interpreted that he might have contradictory thoughts about Daddy. Although Richard knew that Daddy was a kind man, at night when he was frightened, he might fear that Daddy was doing some harm to Mummy. When he thought of the tramp, he did not remember that Daddy, who was in the bedroom with Mummy, would protect her; and that was, Mrs. K. suggested, because he felt it was Daddy himself who might hurt Mummy. (At that moment Richard looked impressed and evidently accepted the interpretation.) In day-time he thought Daddy was nice, but at night when he, Richard, could not see his parents and did not know what they were doing in bed, he might have felt that Daddy was bad and dangerous and that all the terrible things which happened to Cook . . . were happening to Mummy. . . . Just now he had spoken of the terrible things that the Austrian Hitler did to the Austrians. By this he meant that the Austrian Hitler was in a way ill-treating his own people, including Mrs. K., just as the bad Daddy would ill-treat Mummy.[28]

Klein had charged ahead, mobilizing Richard's anxieties: she had opened up the whole area of his fears at night and his worries about his mother and about whether or not he could protect her.

From the very first session, then, Klein was on the lookout for depressive anxiety. Paranoid fears turned up as well. Material of this sort emerged in the twenty-seventh session. Richard asked his analyst, not for the first time, whether she spoke Austrian – he refused to refer to the language as German:

> *Mrs. K.* interpreted that he had . . . shown how much he distrusted her and her son as foreigners and potential spies. They also stood for the unknown Mummy and Daddy, the parents who had secrets, particularly sexual ones, and he felt he could not know whether Mummy contained the Hitler-Daddy. When he was not with his parents, he often distrusted them and he thought that Mummy would give him away to Daddy. . . .
>
> Suddenly and with determination he said that he wanted to tell Mrs. K. something which was worrying him very much. He was afraid of being poisoned by Cook or Bessie [the maid]. They would do this to him because he was often horrid or cheeky to them. From time to time he had a good look at the food to find out whether it was poisoned. He looked into bottles in the kitchen to see what they contained; they might have poison in them which Cook would mix with his food. Sometimes he thought that Bessie . . . was a German spy. He occasionally listened at the key-hole to find out whether Cook and Bessie were speaking German together. (Both Cook and Bessie were British and did not know a word of German, as I subsequently ascertained.) He obviously forced himself to tell all this, looking tortured and worried. . . . He said that these fears made him very unhappy and asked if Mrs. K. could help him with them. . . .
>
> *Mrs. K.* interpreted that he distrusted not only Cook and Bessie but also his parents because he wished to blow them up with his "big job" as well as to poison them with his urine, both of which were felt to be poisonous when he hated his parents. . . . His main fear and guilt came from his unconscious desires to attack them with urine and faeces, to devour and kill them.[29]

In Richard's case Klein dealt sporadically with this kind of material; she failed to treat it as central. Yet as her interpretation indicates, she did have a theoretical framework for thinking about paranoid fears. Simply put, *lex talionis* ruled: Richard's sadistic impulses toward his mother, impulses to attack her breasts as part objects by biting and scooping, with the intention of stealing their food, and to attack the mother as a whole object to rob her of her beauty, babies, and internal penises, provoked a dread of retaliation.

Klein was not to rest content with that law. In her work after the Second World War she shifted her emphasis from depressive anxieties to more primitive paranoid processes.

*   *   *

"In the course of working out my concept of the infantile depressive position," Klein wrote, "the problems of the phase preceding it" – what she called the paranoid-schizoid – "forced themselves on my attention."[30] In so doing, she found herself grappling, albeit gingerly, with problems that heretofore she had managed to avoid: problems of structure. Above all, she felt obliged to look hard at the ego. (Up to this point, among Freud's triad, only the superego had figured prominently in her work; as for the id, it rarely put in an appearance.)

Once again, Klein focused on fantasy, in this instance on one reported by Dr. Daniel Paul Schreber – the subject of Freud's "Psycho-Analytic Notes on an Autobiographical Account of a Case of Paranoia (Dementia Paranoides)" (1911).

> At the climax of his illness, under the influence of visions which were "partly of a terrifying character, but partly, too, of an indescribable grandeur," Schreber became convinced of the imminence of a great catastrophe, of the end of the world. Voices told him that the work of the past 14,000 years had now come to nothing, and that the earth's allotted span was only 212 years more; . . . [subsequently he became convinced] that that period had already elapsed. He himself was the "only real man left alive," and the few human shapes that he still saw – the doctor, the attendants, the other patients – he explained as being "miracled up, cursorily improvised men."[31]

Freud and Klein agreed that Schreber's "end of the world" delusion represented "the projection of . . . [an] internal catastrophe";[32] she described it in terms of "anxieties and phantasies about inner destruction and ego-disintegration."[33] (Even more than Freud, Klein shifted back and forth between "ego" as some sort of psychical agency and "ego" as self.) What "abnormal changes in the ego" brought about paranoid hallucinations such as Schreber's – this was the question that intrigued her.

Two ideas emerged as central in her paper "Notes on Some Schizoid Mechanisms" (1946): splitting and projective identification, and of the two splitting ranked as the schizoid mechanism par excellence. On this subject Freud had left behind only a few brief remarks, set down late in life. His emphasis fell on the splitting off of ideas or the disavowing of pieces of reality: the persistence of "two attitudes . . . side by side . . . without influencing each other" might "rightly be called a splitting of the ego."[34] Elsewhere: "two contrary reactions" to instinctual conflict – the first, continuance of satisfaction, the second, compliance with a prohibition against such a satisfaction – persisted "as the centre-point of a splitting of the ego."[35] Klein's notions were far more concrete. "Splitting of the ego," she argued, resulted in the feeling that the ego was "in bits"; it amounted "to a state of disintegration."[36]

When Klein had written of splitting in connection with the depressive position, it had been splitting of the object that she had had in mind. When she turned from object to ego, and advanced the additional claim that the ego was "incapable of splitting the object – internal and external – without a corresponding splitting taking place in the ego itself," she also moved from projection to projective identification. Projection operated on qualities or properties like anger and love; in contrast, projective identification operated on things or bits of things – more specifically, on split off parts of the self:

> [S]plit-off parts of the ego, . . . expelled in hatred, . . . are . . . projected on to the mother, or as I would rather call it, *into* the mother. These . . . bad parts of the self are meant not only to injure but also to control and take possession of the object.
>
> Much of the hatred against parts of the self is now directed towards the mother. This leads to a particular form of identification which establishes the prototype of an aggressive object-relation. I suggest for these processes the term "projective identification."

In this fashion the split-off parts of the self came to be lodged in an external object. Not literally. Klein did not think that the patient literally put things into another's mind or body. Once more it was a question of the patient's fantasy:

> The processes I have described are, of course, bound up with the infant's phantasy-life; and the anxieties which stimulate the mechanism of splitting are also of a phantastic nature. It is in phantasy that the infant splits . . . the self, but the effect of the phantasy is a very real one, because it leads to feelings and relations . . . being cut off from one another.[37]

*   *   *

What about guilt? Theoretically Klein posited a difference between depressive and persecutory anxiety, between concern for the other and concern for the self – a difference that later generations for Kleinians have continued to regard as crucial. But also as artificial. In her "Note on Depression in the Schizophrenic" (1960), Klein commented:

In the past I have laid emphasis on the distinction between paranoid anxiety, which I defined as being centred on the preservation of the ego, and depressive anxiety, which focuses on the good internalized and external object. As I see it now, this distinction is too schematic.

She phrased her next remarks in terms of diagnostic categories:

I have for many years put forward the view that from the beginning of post-natal life the internalization of the object is the basis of development. This implies that some internalization of the good object also occurs in the paranoid schizophrenic. From birth onwards, however, in an ego lacking in strength and subjected to violent splitting processes the internalization of the good object differs in nature and strength from that of the manic-depressive. It is less permanent, less stable, and does not allow for a sufficient identification with it. Nevertheless, since some internalization of the object does occur, anxiety on behalf of the ego – that is to say, paranoid anxiety – is bound to include some concern for the object.[38]

Then why was guilt so difficult to detect? Here Klein reminded her readers of Schreber, more particularly of his "capacity to divide himself into sixty souls." Given "the violence with which this splitting takes place in the schizophrenic, depressive anxiety and guilt are very strongly split off. Whereas paranoid anxiety is experienced in most parts of the split ego and therefore predominates, guilt and depression are only experienced in some parts which are felt by the schizophrenic to be out of reach" – out of reach, that is, "until the analysis brings them into consciousness."

[I]n the analysis of deep layers of the mind . . . we come across the schizophrenic feelings of despair about being confused and in bits. Further work enables us in some cases to get access to the feelings of guilt and depression about being dominated by destructive impulses and about having destroyed oneself and one's good object by splitting processes. As a defence against such pain we might find that fragmentation occurs again; it is only by repeated experiences of such pain and the analysis of it that progress can be made.[39]

Omnipotence holding sway

Recall Joan Riviere's discussion of a manic defensive system. Following in the wake of Klein's 1935 paper on manic-depressive states, she stressed how such a system operated as a "disguise to conceal . . . a more or less depressive condition in the patient."[40] Following in the wake of Klein's 1946 paper on schizoid mechanisms, successive cohorts of Kleinians highlighted defenses

– elaborated into pathological organizations – against anxieties of the paranoid-schizoid position as well. The relevance of this body of work to a Kleinian account of morality is this: it speaks to the question of why guilt, regarded as inescapable, appears to have gone missing. The very insistence by the Kleinians that paranoid anxieties included some concern for the object made the seeming non-existence of guilt an acute theoretical and technical problem for them.

At this point I could draw on a number of texts to make vivid and graphic the guilt-denying function of pathological organizations. For the sake of clarity, I am focusing on two, one by Hanna Segal, a leading member of the group of Kleinians that emerged soon after the Second World War, and another by John Steiner, who ranks as a prominent third generation Kleinian. They both fastened on perversion – understood as Steiner recommended it be understood – as persistence in error, as a turning away from the truth, with sexual perversion figuring "as a special instance of a more general . . . attitude."[41]

*   *   *

Toward the end of her article, "A Delusional System as a Defence Against the Re-emergence of a Catastrophic Situation" (1972), Segal wondered whether her patient "should . . . have had psychoanalysis at all." She offered an uncertain "yes." In contrast, when it came to the question of research, her affirmative was unequivocal. Although her patient was extremely disturbed, in her view many features of the "psychopathological constellation" she described could be found in less ill patients.[42] She reminded her readers of Freud's belief, voiced as he reflected on Schreber's memoirs, that a psychoanalyst should approach delusions "with a suspicion that even thought-structures so extraordinary as these and so remote from our common modes of thinking" sprang from understandable "impulses of the human mind." Like Freud, Segal insisted that the psychoanalyst would want to go "deeply into the details of the delusion and into the history of its development." But she differed with him as to the nature of the catastrophic situation at the core of her patient's personality. The withdrawal of "libidinal cathexis . . . from the people in his environment" – Freud's hypothesis – did not cover the dynamics of her patient's delusional system.[43] Segal, like Klein, couched the matter in terms of "anxieties and phantasies about inner destruction and ego-disintegration."[44]

Segal's patient was obsessional as well as delusional. "In the first consultation" he told her that "he suffered from severe obsessional ceremonies and from an inability to make up his mind." How serious these symptoms were, Segal found out only in the course of the analysis. To wit: "[H]e could take nine or ten hours to get through his ceremonial before going to bed. In the early days of his analysis he once spent twelve hours making up his mind whether it was more efficient to take a bath before work or to do his work first and take his bath after." But the obsessions themselves had not prompted him to seek treatment; rather it was because they interfered with his mission – "a mission . . . to convert people to Christianity. He had undergone a conversion in which he became convinced that he was a very special chosen instrument of God. To perform his mission he must be perfectly efficient," and his obsessions compromised his efficiency. "He would need to be cured in under four years because otherwise he would be too old to enter a seminary and be ordained. His age was then 44."[45]

The content of the mission was generally quite vague. Segal gathered that it had to do with conversion and that because of her patient's "special strategic genius," the mission itself was "to be strategic, something like becoming the great strategist of the Church of England." In line with this self-image, the patient led his life as a series of what he called "operations." For example: "recapitulation."

> He [the patient] thinks he has got the power to recall in detail every conversation and event that he considers important. At the beginning of his analysis, every analytical hour was followed by what he called "post-analysis," which usually took place in the lavatory and which consisted of a complete recapitulation of everything that was said in the session. This was much more important to him than the analytical session he had with me [Segal].

Another example: "inspirationalism."

> Inspirationalism consists of thinking about, and identifying with, very idealized figures. Usually they are . . . martial figures – Genghis Khan, Churchill, John Kennedy. Inspirationalism consists of a sort of long meditation about the hero and trying to "introject" (his word!) him. For instance, on the radio there was a recording of Churchill's old speeches, and at that time he would miss as much as three days of analysis out of five because he would be either listening . . . or recapitulating . . . the speeches.

These two counted as permanent operations. There were ad hoc ones as well:

> "Operation T" (for which he wanted to take a sabbatical year off the analysis) consists in manipulating and bribing people to get an intro-duction to a professor of history, T. In the meantime the patient has to read and memorize all his works to make a good impression on him; the aim is to have one conversation with the professor and get out of him ideas on how to reform the Church of England.

Taken together, the "operations . . . formed a system in which the patient lived as almost completely omnipotent and controlling his environment, and almost totally shielded from contact with reality."[46]

No wonder, then, that the patient viewed analysis as a serious threat. He would announce to Segal: "You are a saboteur – in wartime saboteurs are shot." And in similar vein, aware that his analyst was Jewish, he would say coldly: "Hitler knew how to deal with you people." As Segal saw it, "the main problem of his analysis from the start . . . was . . . to find links with his infantile self and the infantile transference, particularly the positive transference. There were some slender threads one could follow in that direction, . . . but in the first years of his analysis his defences against recognition of his infantile needs were formidable." In the fifth year of the treatment, Segal noted a promising development:

[T]here emerged in the analysis a part of him which he called "baby Georgie." . . . He had a dream in which a big black dog was chasing – with intent to kill – a tiny little dog. He himself kills the little dog to spare him the suffering. His own associations led us to interpret the dream in this way: the little dog was the normal baby George . . .; the big black dog he called "delusional Georgie." . . . I pointed out to him that what he considers his conscious, adult self also turns against the little dog and, though he does it out of pity, in effect he sides with the big dog. . . . [A]t that time in his analysis he still mostly sided with the operations, and consciously deplored any insight which might interfere with them. . . . The struggle we always had to establish the analysis in the face of the "operations" became more clearly a struggle to rescue "baby Georgie" from "delusional Georgie" a struggle for the survival of what remained of a healthy infantile ego.[47]

Here Segal's knowledge of her patient's early years fed into her understanding of his internal world.

[H]e was breast-fed for about six weeks and he had an extremely traumatic weaning. It was 1917, and when his soldier father came on leave his mother weaned him in order not to spoil the father's leave. There is a letter from his mother to his father saying, "George cried for the breast but I didn't give it to him." Not long after, his father was killed in the war. In the analysis we reconstructed that his mother must have been very depressed and also that some time after his father's death she left him and the family for several months – he thinks, in order to do nursing in France. Around the age of 1 year or 18 months he nearly died of pneumonia, but we do not know whether it was during his mother's absence or after her return. There is a photograph of him aged about 2, sitting in the pram with a completely vacuous expression. At that time an aunt was afraid that he was mentally deficient, because he would sit in his pram for hours without movement or expression.

His mother remarried and his brother was born when he was about 4. There is also a sister three years older. The whole family is very disturbed. Of his natural father we know little, as he is intensely idealized by the whole family as the romantic hero who perished in the war. There are, however, occasional hints of hypochondriacal and obsessional symptoms. The sister was either a severe obsessional or a simple schizophrenic. She was certainly quite incapable of independent existence and up to her death (while the patient was in analysis) lived at home. Like my patient, she had a religious obsession, but without his grandiosity. . . . His younger half-brother, certainly the sanest member of the family, was expelled from school for stealing boys' underwear. . . . Unlike my patient, he is capable to work and had a spell in the Foreign Office; but for years now he has been acting as housekeeper/cook/ nursemaid to his aged mother. The mother, intensely idealized by the whole family, was a beauty in her youth and at times appears as a monster of narcissism. She is completely oblivious of the illness of all her children and quite content to have them at home adoring her. . . . The stepfather, though obsessional and peculiar in many ways, appears as a very much healthier man than the patient's mother or father, and certainly gave my patient as a boy considerable care and devotion.

Segal readily granted an etiological significance to her patient's childhood experience: "his megalomanic delusion and the complex obsessional system needed to maintain it" defended "him against a recurrence of an early catastrophic situation, the abrupt weaning and the subsequent loss of both parents."[48]

But she added an important caveat:

[T]his megalomanic obsessional system itself became in fact a chronic catastrophe. It is the existence of the system that prevented him from making contact with such aspects of his mother as were available to him and from renewing any real contact with her after her return. It prevented him from benefiting sufficiently from the paternal kindness of his stepfather or the devotion that both his siblings had for him. Baby Georgie and his potential for growth were stunted not by the "catastrophe" but by the delusional system developed to prevent . . . [its] recurrence.

At one and the same time as the system entailed "the ceaseless exploitation" of the patient's "real external objects and the ceaseless projection of painful feelings, denied in himself, onto them," and stood as a "complete bulwark against guilt."

> When he started analysis it was clear that he had never in his life experienced a feeling of guilt. He lies, cheats and steals without compunction. He also finds it hard to visualize that other people may have different standards. He is always shocked and bewildered if someone refuses a bribe. . . . [H]e told me that it does not matter if he seduces a thousand boys if it does him good, since he might in the end be able to save a million souls.[49]

*   *   *

At the close of her paper, Segal reported positively on the analysis:

> The "operations" – though by no means abandoned – are clearly felt by him now as a symptom and have been much curtailed in time and intensity. In his relationships he seems much more human. He sometimes expresses affection for me now, and gratitude that I did not let him destroy the analysis.[50]

Segal obviously hoped against hope that her patient would be able to dismantle or loosen his rigid structure and begin to experience love and concern for his objects – and *a fortiori* guilt as well. The trajectory Steiner described in his article "The Retreat from Truth to Omnipotence in Sophocles's *Oedipus at Colonus*" (1990) was just the reverse: from the experience of guilt to the construction of a defensive system. For his material, as his title indicates, he turned to literature rather than to his consulting room – appreciating full well that such material invited a radical, and useful, simplification.[51]

Steiner took as his point of departure a novel reading of *Oedipus the King*. (He freely acknowledged drawing on the work of "an idiosyncratic classicist," Philip Vellacott.)[52] It goes like this:

> [F]ar from being ignorant and hence innocent of what he did, . . . Oedipus must have realized that he had killed Laius and married his widow. He arrived in Thebes having just killed a man who was evidently important . . . and must have found the city buzzing with news of the death of the king. It is true that both he and everyone else was preoccupied with the threat of the Sphinx, but it is impossible to think that he did not connect these events. He solved the riddle of the Sphinx and accepted the hand of Jocasta because . . . the desire to enjoy Laius's throne and Jocasta's bed made him a poor logician.
>   Later he asks why there was no inquiry into Laius's death, but neither Creon [Jocasta's brother], nor Jocasta nor the Elders wanted to

know. They for their individual reasons preferred to accept the new king and to welcome the overthrow of the Sphinx without asking awkward questions. Later we learn that Tiresias [a blind old prophet] knew and kept the knowledge to himself for seventeen years. It seems . . . clear that . . . an unconscious or half-conscious collusion took place, since if any one of them had exercised . . . [his] curiosity the truth would easily have come out.

Did Oedipus also realize that Laius was his father and Jocasta his mother? This was perhaps not so obvious, and yet the play is riddled with hints that could and should have been followed up. In order to maintain that he is the son of Polybus and Merope, Oedipus turns a blind eye to the fact that he went to consult the Oracle precisely because he had doubts about his parentage which the Oracle did nothing to allay. With the prophecy [that he will murder his father and wed his mother] ringing in his ears he kills a man old enough to be his father and marries a woman old enough to be his mother.[53]

Here Steiner quoted the observations of "an unusual theatre director":

My dear, I am sorry to say this, but no one has understood before now that *Oedipus* is not about the revelation of truth but about the cover-up of truth. Everybody knows who Oedipus is from the start and everybody is covering up. Just like Watergate. Just like all through history – the lie is what societies are based on.[54]

At the climax of the play, everything is disclosed. Thereupon Jocasta commits suicide, and Oedipus, using his mother/wife's brooches as weapons, blinds himself. How are we to understand the self-blinding? It has usually been said that Oedipus puts his eyes out because he recognizes that he has lived among illusions, that all along he has been blind. Vellacott adds a "further twist of the screw." The illusion which his "'aware Oedipus' has cherished is that he can live his life on the basis of a belief which is almost certainly false . . .; that he can assert ignorance and innocence in face of multiple evidence. . . . His sin was the corrupting of his own power of knowledge, the enthroning of an illusion in the place of truth. . . . The retribution did not reach his inner self until he saw Iocasta lying dead. . . . [A]nd the self-punishment that follows shows moral perception fully re-established."[55]

In *Oedipus at Colonus*, written roughly two decades later, Sophocles takes the story up again. Having been banished from Thebes at his own request (something which he misrepresents time after time) Oedipus, now a blind old man, is wandering in the vicinity of Athens, looking for a place to die. His two daughters, Antigone and Ismene, are devoted to him: Antigone, by his side, guiding and supporting him; Ismene, at home, looking after his interests there. In contrast, his two sons, Eteocles and Polyneices, have refused to help their father and are about to fight each other for power in Thebes. Eteocles remains in the city with Creon, while Polyneices retreats to Argos, where he assembles an army.

Here is a synopsis of the plot. Oedipus reaches Colonus and stumbles into a sacred grove. The elders are horrified that he has entered hallowed ground and even more horrified when they find out who he is, his past being well known. They insist that he leave; he, in turn, insists that he is a holy man who will bring great advantage to Athens. Theseus, its king, is sent for. In the meantime Ismene appears bringing news of the conflict between her brothers, bringing news also of a fresh decree from Dephi declaring that whoever provides a sanctuary for Oedipus's grave will be favored by the gods and protected in battle. When Theseus arrives, he accepts Oedipus's offer of his body and, in exchange, promises a shrine within the sacred grove. Thesus then exits. Now Creon enters the scene, lays claim to Oedipus, tries to take him by force, having already abducted his daughters. Theseus returns, saves Oedipus, and frees Antigone and Ismene. Next Polyneices comes to plead with his father and is firmly rebuffed. Finally Oedipus prepares himself for death. Only Theseus is to know where he is buried, and this secret will be handed down to successive generations of Athenian kings.

The Oedipus of this drama is far different from the figure of the earlier tragedy. As Steiner put it: "We no longer see a man who could acknowledge his guilt and who is shattered . . .; instead we meet a haughty, arrogant man who makes repeated and devious self-excuses." Oedipus does not deny the facts. But the facts, he insists, point to his having been sinned against rather than to his having sinned. This is a man "who in taking on divine characteristics sheds the very humanity he fought hard to achieve, . . . who adopts a superior grandeur and relates to others . . . with coldness and cruelty."[56] Nowhere does this coldness and cruelty – a deluded self-righteousness – come out more forcefully than in his response to Polyneices:

> Well: he has asked, and he shall hear from me
> A kind of answer that will not overjoy him.
> You scoundrel!
>   When it was you who held
> Throne and authority – as your brother now
> Holds them in Thebes – you drove me into exile:
> Me, your own father: made me a homeless man. . . .
>
> You cannot take that city. You'll go down
> All bloody, and your brother, too.
>   For I
> Have placed that curse upon you before this,

And now I invoke that curse to fight for me,
That you may see a reason to respect
Your parents, though your birth was as it was;
And though I am blind, not to dishonor me. . . .

And so your supplication and your throne
Are overmastered surely, – if accepted
Justice still has place in the laws of God.
Now go! For I abominate and disown you
You utter scoundrel! Go with the malediction
I have pronounced for you: that you shall never
Master your native land by force of arms,
Nor ever see your home again in Argos,
The land below the hills; but you shall die
By your brother's hand, and you shall kill
The brother who banished you. For this I pray.[57]

In Steiner's judgment, the changes in Oedipus amount to a retreat from truth to omnipotence. Oedipus, now blind, turns to divine authority – to the gods who had singled him out to perpetrate the most awful deeds and who now promise to make him a hero and elevate him to the status of a near god. Allied with such all-mighty figures, Oedipus simply dismisses reality – and guilt. Gods are familiar with wrath; culpability is foreign to them.

*   *   *

Recall Klein's 6-year-old patient Erna, more particularly recall her extravagant sadistic fantasies and how persecuted she felt. Sadism and its projection – emphasized by Klein in the late 1920s – was intellectual property Freud acknowledged sharing with her. So too he acknowledged as part of his theoretical armamentarium the inference she had drawn from Erna's material and that of other child patients: they had internalized a grossly distorted object from whom nothing but hostility could be expected.

Freud admitted his debt in *Civilization and Its Discontents*, and his 1930 text provided the starting point for this chapter – a further exploration of guilt and its vicissitudes. He pointedly asked how civilization "set limits to man's aggressive instincts" and held "the manifestations of them in check." In response he offered a thorough-going account of the superego and the painful feelings it engendered. Indeed it often outdid itself: it treated the ego with an unnecessary ferocity. Freud hypothesized – in line with Klein – that the superego entered "into possession of all the aggressiveness which the child would have liked to exercise" against the original authority figure.[38]

Having contended with sadism and the paranoid fears it begot in the 1920s, Klein postponed a further reckoning. Instead she brought ambivalence front and center – emphasizing its loving side – and worked out the concept of the depressive position – a concept that was unavailable to Freud. With her subsequent formulation of the paranoid-schizoid position, she took up persecution once more. As for splitting (whence "schizoid"), that too had been a staple of her thinking. Following W. R. D. Fairbairn, she added – and it was no small addition – splitting of the ego to her earlier ideas about splitting of the object. Splitting itself came coupled with another mechanism: projective identification. Taken together they suggested an even more dynamic and certainly more complexly organized inner world than had previously been thought. By the same token the possible disguises guilt might assume or possible hiding places it might lurk increased in number.

It was Segal and Steiner, who, thanks in large measure to their work with seriously disturbed patients, explored such pathological retreats. They discovered that in their detail pathological organizations remained idiosyncratic constructions, archives of personal history and personal meaning. A couple of general features, however, emerged. Here they found a destructive superego domiciled without being domesticated. Here too they found omnipotence of thought run rampant. Willy-nilly questions of moral and cognitive development became entwined.

Chapter 4

The ego gaining ground

The two previous chapters ended with omnipotence of thought figuring as critical to a person's defending against, warding off, in short, evading unbearable guilt. In this chapter omnipotent defenses are not confronted head on. Instead I have taken a cue from Hamlet: "By indirections find directions out." If, as a possible outcome of treatment, a patient becomes more realistic, as a corollary or by-product, omnipotence will lose its hold.

Let's return, then, to the reality principle – something Freud had spelled out in "Formulations on the Two Principles of Mental Functioning" (1911). As a regulatory principle of mental functioning, it emerged secondarily. The pleasure principle came first and was initially dominant; and even the transition from it to the reality principle did not entail suppression – the sexual instincts, for their part, were belatedly and incompletely educated. In similar vein, "*phantasying*," which began "already in children's play, . . . was kept free from reality-testing and . . . continued as *day-dreaming*."[1] More than a decade later, in *The Ego and the Id* (1923), Freud made the ego responsible for assuring obedience to the reality principle. The ego sought "to bring the influence of the external world to bear upon the id and its tendencies" and endeavored "to substitute the reality principle for the pleasure principle" which reigned "unreservedly in the id."[2]

The id made only fleeting appearances in Melanie Klein's writings; fantasy held center stage – more particularly the unconscious variety. That fantasy might be unconscious certainly fit with Freud's way of thinking: like an incompatible idea or a painful memory, it could be repressed.[3] Could there also be a species of fantasy that had never been conscious at all? Freud answered in the affirmative; yet most of his remarks "give the impression that he thought unconscious phantasies . . . were like islands in the sea of mental life. Reading Klein's work with children, one gets a glimpse of an internal phantasy world like a vast continent under the sea, the islands being its conscious, external, observable manifestations."[4] This extension of Freud's concept of fantasy and this insistence on its importance, prompted Klein to reconsider the reality principle and to reject Freud's account of its emergence as a simple progression.

It was her followers, chiefly Hanna Segal and Wilfred R. Bion, who carried forward the reconsideration. Both were in treatment with Klein when she published her 1946 paper, "Notes on Some Schizoid Mechanisms." Both took off from her conceptualization of the paranoid-schizoid position. To Klein's depiction of movement between the paranoid-schizoid and depressive positions, Segal added and elaborated a cognitive dimension. Bion was more ambitious. He introduced a thirst for knowledge and put it on a par with love and hate. (In the 1920s Klein had been concerned with what, following Freud, she had referred to as the epistemophilic instincts. Then her interest in them had fallen off. So Bion's introduction could be regarded as a reintroduction.) He also reintroduced the mother, more specifically, as container – as someone able to take in the infant's feelings and make them bearable. Where Klein had written of the introjection of a good object as crucial for emotional growth, Bion wrote of the introjection of an understanding object as crucial for the growth of one capacity in particular, that of learning from experience.

Drawing on Bion's work, Betty Joseph and Ronald Britton – neither of whom had been analyzed by Klein, but were influenced by her as well as by Bion – concentrated on the experience and the learning that could occur in the consulting room, on changes in ego functioning that analytic therapy might produce. Joseph, in her clinical practice, searched for that part of the patient's ego that "was able moment to moment" to take an interest in understanding. She regarded "the strengthening of this part of the personality" as crucial[5] – and feasible. Britton in similar vein, considered how a person's growing ability to face reality – understood as internal or psychic as well as external or material – made possible his emancipation from a punitive superego and his reclaiming a right to pass judgment on himself.

Principles of mental functioning

Of all the topics canvassed during the Controversial Discussions, none produced more heat than unconscious fantasy.[6] In Paula Heimann's paper on introjection and projection (discussed in Chapter 2) these two mechanisms stood as particular instances of fantasy at work. Susan Isaacs addressed the more general phenomenon in the very first paper of the series, "The Nature and Function of Phantasy." On behalf of the Kleinians she launched a campaign aimed at securing the notion of psychical reality.

Freud's discovery of that reality, Isaacs insisted, marked a new epoch for psychology, and fantasy, implicitly understood as "*unconscious* mental content, which may seldom or never become conscious," ranked as the key term – and one that was subject to misconstrual.

> [T]he word "phantasy" is often used in contrast to "reality," the latter word being taken as identical with "external" or "material" or

"objective" facts. But when external reality is called "objective" reality, there is an assumption which denies to psychical reality its own objectivity as a mental fact. Some analysts tend to contrast "phantasy" with "reality" in such a way as to undervalue the dynamic importance of phantasy. A related usage is to think of "phantasy" as something "merely" or "only" imagined, as something unreal, in contrast to what is actual, what happens *to* me. Both these attitudes have the significance of underrating the psychical reality and meaning of mental processes as such.[7]

As Klein and her co-workers saw it, Freud had found a way into a fascinating and mysterious world, but had not fully appreciated his own discoveries[8] – and as a consequence, stalemate, or worse, retreat loomed as a threat.

With her claim that "unconscious phantasies are the primary content of all mental processes," Isaacs went on the offensive:

Phantasy is the mental corollary, the psychic representative of instinct. And there is no impulse, no instinctual urge, which is not represented as (unconscious) phantasy. . . .

Phantasy expresses the specific content of the urge (or the feeling, e.g., hate, anxiety, fear, love, or sorrow) which is dominating to the child's mind at the moment, e.g., when he feels desires towards his mother, he experiences these as "I want to suck the nipple, to stroke her face, to eat her up, to keep her inside me, to bite the breast, to tear her to bits, to drown and burn her, to throw her out of me" and so on and so forth.

When he feels anxiety, stirred up by an aggressive wish, he feels, "I shall be bitten or cut up by my mother." When he feels loss and grief, he experiences . . . , "My mother has gone forever." He may feel, "I want to bring her back," and try to overcome his sense of loss and grief by the phantasy "I shall bring her back by stroking my genital," when he masturbates. When he wants to restore his mother, he feels "I want to make her better, to feed her, to put the bits together again" and so on. . . .

Moreover, . . . he not only feels "I want to" but actually "*I am doing*" this and that action towards his mother. This is the omnipotent character of early mental processes, when the wish is felt as the deed.[9]

In advancing this broad concept of fantasy and postulating its appearance practically at birth, Isaacs went well beyond Freud. Ernest Jones, for one, reacted positively. He was the first discussant to enter the fray, and he lent Isaacs his support:

The stress she [Isaacs] lays . . . on the apprehension of psychical reality, and the debt we here owe to Freud, is quite fundamental. I would say that the hall-mark of psychoanalysts is their feeling for unconscious psychical reality, and I agree with her remark that even among psychoanalysts this feeling is often not so highly developed as it might be – despite vocal assertions to the contrary.

As for Isaacs's expansion of fantasy, that too he backed up:

The cry may be raised that she has changed the meaning of a familiar word, but I do not think so. I am reminded of a similar situation years ago with the word "sexuality." The critics complained that Freud was changing the meaning of this word, and Freud himself once or twice seemed to assent to this way of putting it, but I always protested that he made no change in the meaning of the word itself; what he did was to extend the conception and, by giving it a fuller content, to make it more comprehensive. This process would seem to be inevitable in psychoanalytical work, since many conceptions, e.g., that of conscience which were previously known only in their conscious sense, must be widened when we add to this their unconscious significance. Mrs. Isaacs' procedure is therefore fully justified in the light of psycho-analytical development.[10]

Jones was hopeful that by concentrating on clinical examples and comparing "alternative explanations of them with the aim of ascertaining which of these most closely" covered "the facts," the members of the society might reach agreement.[11] He hoped in vain. The consulting room, and reports of its goings-on, failed to settle disputes among rival concepts; it proved more serviceable in inspiring novel ideas.

* * *

So it had been with Klein, and so she made clear as early as the 1920s with the first written accounts she provided of her work. She depicted how she engaged her young patients, particularly her son Erich, alias Fritz, and managed to elicit from them their thoughts and feelings.[12] That one might analyze one's own child was broadly accepted in Klein's professional milieu; it was done by other psychoanalysts and even considered the correct procedure with children. With Freud's Little Hans, for example, the treatment was conducted by the boy's father. Indeed Freud was of the opinion that "no one else . . . could have prevailed on the child" to avow his fanciful notions. "It was only because the authority of a father and physician were united in a single person, and because in him affectionate care and scientific interest were combined, that it was possible . . . to apply the [psychoanalytic] method to a use to which it would not have otherwise lent itself."[13] Klein was very shortly to disagree with Freud, to become "absolutely firm" on "keeping parental influence . . . apart from analysis" and reducing it to "its minimum."[14] But with Fritz she seemed to use Freud's "Analysis of a Phobia in a Five-Year-Old Boy" as childrearing guide and treatment manual alike.

What about her son, when he was roughly the same age as Little Hans, prompted Klein to intervene analytically in his upbringing?

> The boy was suffering from a play-inhibition that went hand in hand with an inhibition against listening to or telling stories. There was an increasing taciturnity, hypercriticalness, absent-mindedness and unsociableness. Although the child's mental condition as a whole could not at this stage have been described as an "illness," still one is justified in making assumptions . . . about possible developments. These inhibitions as regards play, story-telling, listening, and further, the hypercriticalness about trifles and absent-mindedness, might at a later stage have developed into neurotic traits of character. . . . [T]he peculiarities indicated here had to some degree been present – though not so noticeably – since the child was very small; it was only as they developed and others were added that they afforded the more striking impression that led to my regarding the interference of psychoanalysis as advisable.[15]

Klein reported on this "interference" over a number of papers, and the treatment itself took place in four distinct periods.[16] During the first two Klein provided a good deal of education, principally enlightening Fritz about the facts of life. In the second two, she approached the material without so clear an agenda or game-plan; instead she tracked Fritz's anxiety, taking its diminution as a sign that she was "working on the right lines."[17] More and more she was struck by the extent to which the child's life was dominated by unconscious fantasy.

"At the age of four and three quarters, questions concerning birth set in," and with them the first period – roughly a week – of therapy. Klein answered her son "absolutely truthfully and, when necessary, on a scientific basis suited to his understanding, but as briefly as possible." Along with queries about birth "went a striking increase" in Fritz's inquisitiveness in general. For example: "'Where was I before I was born?'" Or: "'How is a person made?'" Klein "repeated the explanation given him often before." The "knowledge was . . . not easily assimilated" – and the questions did not cease. Once again Fritz asked: "Mamma, please, how did you come into the world?" The decisive conversation, in Klein's view, concerned the existence, or non-exitence, of God. It occurred after a rainy day.

> Quite spontaneously he [Fritz] . . . asked, "It isn't God who made the rain? Toni" (the maid) "said that God made the rain! . . . Is it only a story that God makes the rain?" On her [Klein's] replying in the affirmative, he continued, "But there really is God?" His mother replied a little evasively that she had never seen him. "One doesn't see him but he is really up in the sky?" – "In the sky there are only air and clouds" – . . . "But there is really God," he asked again. There was no escape; so she came to a decision and said, "No, child, he is not real."

On this subject Klein and her husband differed. He considered himself a pantheist, and when Fritz asked him: "'Papa, is there really a God?'" he simply answered "'Yes.'"

> Fritz retorted, "But mamma said there really is no God." Just at this moment, his mother entered the room and he asked her at once, "Mamma, please, papa says there really is a God. Does God really exist?" She was naturally rather taken aback and answered, "I have never seen him and do not believe . . . that God exists." At this juncture her husband came to her assistance and saved the situation by saying, "Look here, Fritz, no one has ever seen God and some people believe that God exists and others believe that he doesn't." Fritz, who throughout had looked from one to the other with great anxiety, now became quite cheerful and explained, "I think too that there is no God."

The six weeks subsequent to her interventions were marked by intellectual growth, both broad and deep. But these favorable results did not last: Fritz became reserved and disinclined to play. And, coincidentally, he stopped asking questions.What to make of this turn of events? By now Fritz had not only been enlightened about the deity; he had also been told about "the development of the foetus within the maternal body and the birth processes, with all the details which interested him."[18] In this, Klein adhered to her early-established principle of providing information only when explicitly requested – and so the father's part in the sex act remained unexplained. (Freud would have urged further instruction.)[19] She herself surmised that to deal with conscious questions alone "had proved to be insufficient."[20]

Klein looked for a chance to supply the missing facts – and therewith began a second stint of treatment.

> One of his questions at that time so infrequent, namely, which of all the plants grew from seeds, was taken as an opportunity to explain to him that human beings too came from seed and to enlighten him about the act of impregnation. He was absent-minded and inattentive, . . . interrupted the explanation with another irrelevant question and showed

absolutely no desire to inform himself about the details. . . . He gave the distinct impression that he had entirely failed to comprehend this quite new piece of information and that he did not wish to comprehend it.

Klein was disappointed. But she quickly came to appreciate that she should not be misled by a failure to acknowledge information imparted. She persevered. Over the course of subsequent conversations, Fritz let her in on the sexual theories that were occupying him – the notion that children grew in the mother's stomach, that they were made of food and were identical with feces – and gave her another opening.

> He [Fritz] is sitting early in the morning on the chamber, and explains that the kakis are on the balcony, have run upstairs again and don't want to go into the garden (as he repeatedly designated the chamber). I ask him, "These are the children then that grow in the stomach?" As I notice this interests him I continue, "For the kakis are made from the food; real children are not made from food." He, "I know that, they are made of milk." "Oh no, they are made of something that papa makes and the egg that is inside mamma." (He is very attentive now and asks me to explain.) When I begin once more about the little egg, he interrupts me, "I know that." I continue, "Papa can make something with his wiwi that really looks rather like milk and is called seed; he makes it like wiwi only not so much. Mamma's wiwi is different to papa's" (he interrupts) "I know *that*!" I say, "Mamma's wiwi is like a hole. If papa puts his wiwi into mamma's wiwi and makes a seed there, then the seed runs in deeper into her body and when it meets one of the little eggs that are inside mamma, then that little egg begins to grow and it becomes a child." Fritz listened with great interest and said. "I would so much like to see how a child is made inside like that."

Klein was pleased. Fritz had shown curiosity about "the hitherto rejected part of the explanation" and had also shown that he had assimilated it. After roughly two months, the second stint ended or, better, was interrupted. Klein became "indisposed" and was "unable to concern herself with the child." (Additionally political turmoil in postwar Hungary forced her to move from Budapest to Berlin, with a year-long stay in Slovakia en route.) Fritz suffered a setback: "his playing alone and story-telling . . . greatly decreased; . . . he was . . . much naughtier and less cheerful."[21]

A third period, lasting approximately six weeks, was once more broken off because of external circumstances. At last settled in Berlin, the 7-year-old Fritz, now having started school, promptly developed a "great distaste" for it and "for all his tasks." Klein began the fourth and final phase of her son's therapy. Among the tasks assigned him, he found long division the most onerous. He understood the explanations perfectly well, "but always did the sums wrong."

> He told me once that in doing division he had first to bring down the figure that was required and he climbed up, seized it by the arm and pulled it down. To my enquiry as to what it said to that, he replied that quite certainly it was not pleasant for the number – it was as if his mother stood on a stone 13 yards high and someone came and caught her by the arm so that they tore it and divided her. . . . He then related (also in connection with a previously elaborated phantasy) that actually every child wants to have a bit of his mother, who is to be cut in . . . pieces; he depicted . . . how she screamed and had paper stuffed in her mouth so that she could not scream and what kind of faces she made, etc. A child took a very sharp knife, and he described how she was cut up; first across the width of the breast, and then of the belly, then lengthwise so that the "*pipi*" (penis), the face and the head were cut exactly through the middle. . . . He continued that every child then took the piece of the mother that it wanted, and agreed that the cut-up mother was then also eaten. It now appeared also that he always confused the remainder with the quotient in division, and always wrote it in the wrong place, because in his mind it was bleeding pieces of flesh with which he was unconsciously dealing.[22]

Klein appended a footnote: The next day in school both Fritz and his teacher were astonished to find that "he could now do all his sums correctly."[23] Here was an instance where hidden in the child's performance lay the elaboration of an unconscious fantasy. Klein found many another: she conveyed the impression of a rich fantasy life underpinning not just pathological inhibitions but the full range of the child's relations to school and indeed of all his activities.

Had Klein so privileged fantasy that the reality principle stood in danger of being relegated to the status of epiphenomenon? Not until the Controversial Discussions did she feel obliged to confront this issue directly.

*   *   *

In the debate following Isaacs's paper, Marjorie Brierley raised the crucial question of the relation between fantasy-thinking and reality-thinking.

> The wholesale equation of subjective interpretation, meaning, and psychic content with phantasy seems to me to go beyond what is required by the facts. Not that I do not appreciate the cogency of Mrs Isaacs' arguments. . . . I can see that the expansion of the term "phantasy" does simplify and clarify the relationship of later unconscious phantasy to archaic mental experience, but I am not sure it does

not over-simplify. . . . This does not mean that I think pre-verbal phantasy improbable; on general grounds it would appear probable. . . . But if we expand the concept phantasy to cover all primitive subjective experience, we must also extend it forwards and regard all adult thinking, not merely as developed from and continually influenced by, more primitive modes of thinking, but as itself a variety of phantasy.[24]

This question troubled Klein: she was not satisfied with Isaacs's initial response to it; she could not concur in her adherent's contention that thinking "derived from phantasy."[25] And she wrote Isaacs accordingly:

I am now coming to a very important point, which has been on my mind ever since our first discussion about your paper. That refers to the end of your paper. . . . You will remember our discussion in Dr. Heimann's flat about your reply, and that I felt I could not agree to the concept of unconscious phantasy being, as it were, everything to begin with on the mental side. I have felt ever since you wrote your paper, and I am of course fully responsible for your formulation, having shared it and agreed with it – I have felt uncertain about its going too far.

In contrast, Isaacs's remarks "about adaptation to reality starting at the very beginning, and being expressed by the baby's taking the breast or the food" did strike Klein as "convincing." She then added: "But if this is true we would have no right to say that this derives from the Ucs phantasy, but only that it goes along with it."[26] And in her final reply to Brierley, Isaacs took heed: she modified her position, accepted Brierley's distinction between fantasy-thinking and reality-thinking, and suggested that both operated, harnessed together, from birth onward.

In connection with the beginnings of mental functioning, Klein alerted Isaacs to another concern:

Now here is such an excellent point when you proved that it is not possible to divorce . . . intellectual development from object relationship. But I wish you would make it clearer than you do. As it stands, . . . you speak of the building up of object relations, but do not sufficiently prove the point that all these questions of perception etc. cannot be considered divorced from the development of object relations. When you told it to me recently it was more clear than in your paper.[27]

Nothing Isaacs – nor any other participant – said during the Controversial Discussions shed further light. Klein herself had merely hinted at a connection between object relations and cognition, between affective and cognitive development in the early 1930s. After the Second World War,

Segal and Bion picked up Klein's hints as well as her prewar theorizing and made coming to know a subject for psychoanalytic investigation.

Coming to know

In Segal and Bion, Klein found disciples of very different stripes. Of the two, Segal ranked as the more loyal and/or orthodox. Though 21 years Bion's junior – she was born in 1918, he in 1897 – she finished her psychoanalytic training a half-decade before him, in 1945. With her first book, *Introduction to the Work of Melanie Klein* (1964), she became widely recognized as the leading exponent of Klein's ideas.[28] Fashioning a project of her own, she set out to describe how Klein's way of thinking could readily encompass matters central to cognitive development. For his part, Bion appropriated the same concepts, but, in contrast to Segal, stretched them to allow cognitive development an independent status. When it came to reflecting on guilt, Segal returned to Klein's narrative of reparation and working through the depressive position; Bion implicitly suggested a fresh approach, one that hinged less on restoring the object and more on strengthening the ego.

*   *   *

The problems Segal posed, the theoretical tasks she set herself, followed Klein's discussion of fantasy – or rather from her gloss on that discussion. Writing two decades after the Controversial Discussions, Segal skirted the vexed matter of the relation between fantasy-thinking and reality-thinking. On the one hand, she claimed, "phantasy may be considered the psychic representative or the mental correlate, the mental expression of instincts. . . . Since instincts operated from birth, some crude phantasy life can be assumed as existing from birth."

> For example, an infant going to sleep, contentedly making sucking noises and movements with his mouth and sucking his own fingers, phantasies that he is actually sucking or incorporating the breast and goes to sleep with a phantasy of having the milk-giving breast actually inside himself. Similarly, a hungry, raging infant, screaming and kicking, phantasies that he is actually attacking the breast, tearing and destroying it, and experiences his own screams which tear him and hurt him as the torn breast attacking him in his own inside.

On the other hand, she insisted, "from the moment of birth the infant has to deal with the impact of reality, starting with the experience of birth . . . and proceeding to endless experiences of gratification and frustration of his desires. . . . [R]eality . . . exerts a very strong influence on unconscious phantasy itself."

Take, for instance, the infant who is beginning to get hungry and who overcomes hunger by an omnipotent hallucination of having a good feeding breast: his situation will be radically different if he is soon fed from what it will be if he is allowed to remain hungry for a long time. In the first situation the real breast that is offered by the mother will, in the infant's experience, merge with the breast that has been phantasied, and the infant's feeling will be that his own goodness and that of the good object are strong and lasting. In the second case the infant will be overcome by hunger and anger and, in his phantasy, the experience of a bad and persecuting object will become stronger with its implication that his own anger is more powerful than his love and the bad object stronger than the good one.[29]

And so Segal hedged her bets.

At the same time she struck a new note in locating the turning point for cognitive growth in the depressive position. Klein had written of a child forming a concept of a whole object; Segal coupled this achievement with advances in reality testing.

Concern for the object, a leading characteristic of the depressive position, contributes to reality-testing; there is anxious scanning of the object to assess its state. The wish to preserve the integrity of the object . . . leads to an acceptance of reality. . . . As the depressive position gains ascendance there is a progressive diminution of omnipotence and of distortion of perception through projection. . . . [T]he matching of one's own phantasies with the perception of reality . . . can take place.

She summed up: "The shift from the paranoid-schizoid to the depressive position is a fundamental change from psychotic to sane functioning."[30]

Segal's chief interest lay with the psychotic. And in writing about very disturbed patients, she paid close attention to reality thinking, both clinically and conceptually.

*   *   *

In "Some Aspects of the Analysis of a Schizophrenic" (1950), Segal provided background information about her patient Edward.

[He] was a diffident, over-sensitive child and adolescent. Very intellectual and over-ambitious, he was superficially well adapted to his surroundings but, in fact, completely, withdrawn and secretive to the point of obsession. As a child, he was already interested in biology and centered on it all his infantile sexual curiosity and his intellectual interests. . . . At school he got along quite well. Somehow his personality seemed to fit the requirements of the old-fashioned public school. His difficulties went unnoticed by himself as well as by his teachers and schoolfellows. Within the limited field of his interests he was quite brilliant and won a scholarship to a famous college, first among hundreds.

When at the age of eighteen and a half he was called up, things became much more difficult. He was sent to India and went to an Engineers' OCTU [Officer Cadet Training Unit] but could not cope with the training. . . . [He] started to worry obsessively about whether he should remain at the OCTU or resign in the hope of getting released sooner and being able to resume his studies. He became anxious, brooding, and showed signs of an approaching breakdown. Eventually, he resigned impulsively when an officer called him a fool. But he could not bear being a private. . . .

After a few months he was asked to work in a photographic laboratory, in a darkroom, and that seems to have precipitated a complete breakdown. The breakdown began with worry about his eyes going wrong. Then ever-growing delusions appeared. These concerned Chinese plots to take power in India, a biologist wanting to destroy the whole world and so on. He had his first aural hallucinations. At last he wrote a letter to his Colonel denouncing the biologist who wanted to destroy the world, and this led to his being put in a mental hospital.

He spent six months in various military hospitals – six months of "delusions, nightmares, hallucinations," coupled with a "complete loss of feeling of identity, sense of time and place or any continuity in himself or in the world."[31]

It was in those hospitals that Segal had her first, short interviews with him. After his parents had him transferred to a private nursing home, he started an analysis of five hours a week.

In the first session Edward showed no surprise at seeing me [Segal]. He was excited, elated and showed flight of ideas. He told me, in a disconnected way, about the terrifying things done to him in the hospitals by the mad doctors and about the necessity of his being allowed out of this prison immediately. He hoped I would help him to get out. There was no question, at this point, in asking him to lie down on the couch or of explaining to him the nature of the treatment.

But within half a year, he "lay on the couch, associated and, at least consciously, expected nothing" from Segal other than analysis.[32]

From the outset Segal was struck by Edward's difficulty in fashioning symbols – a difficulty that severely hampered his capacity to communicate with his analyst and with himself. She enlarged on this aspect of the case in "Notes of Symbol Formation" (1957).

In the first weeks of his [Edward's] analysis, he came into a session blushing and giggling, and throughout the session would not talk to me. Subsequently we found that before the hour he had been attending an occupational therapy class where he made a canvas stool, which he brought with him. The reason for his silence, blushing and giggling was that he could not bring himself to talk to me about it. For him, the stool on which he had been working, the word "stool" which he would have to use in connection with it, and the stool he passed in the lavatory were so completely felt as one and the same thing that he was unable to talk to me about it. His subsequent analysis revealed that this equation of the three "stools," the word, the chair, and the feces, was at the same time completely unconscious. All he was consciously aware of was that he was embarrassed and could not talk to me.

Edward could use substitutes for an earlier object – which is the crux of symbol formation – but the substitutes were "felt and treated as though they were *identical* with it." For "this non-differentiation between the thing symbolized and the symbol," Segal used the term "symbolic equation." Her classic example came from another schizophrenic patient: "He was once asked by his doctor why he had stopped playing the violin. . . . He replied with some violence, 'Why? Do you expect me to masturbate in public?'"[33] Violin and genital figured as equivalent.

The next step ranked as decisive: "For the sake of clarity," Segal made "a very sharp distinction between the ego's relations [to objects] in the paranoid-schizoid position and in the depressive position . . ., and an equally sharp distinction between the symbolic equations and the symbols which are formed during and after the depressive position."

The chief characteristics of the infant's first object relations are the following. The object is seen as split into an ideally good and wholly bad one. The aim of the ego is total union with the ideal object and total annihilation of the bad one, as well as of the bad parts of the self. . . . A leading defense mechanism in this phase is projective identification. In projective identification, the subject in phantasy projects large parts of himself into the object, and the object becomes identified with the part of the self that it is felt to contain. . . . The differentiation between the self and the object is obscured. Then, since a part of the ego is confused with the object, the symbol – which is a creation of the ego – becomes, in turn, confused with the object which is symbolized.

A dramatic change, she claimed, took place when the depressive position was reached, when there was "a greater . . . awareness . . . of the separateness between the ego and the object," when "the object" was "felt as a whole object."

The ego in this phase is struggling with its ambivalence. Its relation to the object is characterized by guilt, fear of loss or actual experience of loss and mourning, and a striving to re-create the object. . . . This situation is a powerful stimulus for the creation of symbols, and symbols acquire new functions which change their character. The symbol is needed to displace aggression from the original object and, in that way, to lessen the guilt and the fear of loss. . . . [T]he symbol here is not the equivalent of the object. . . . [It] . . . is felt to *represent* the object.[34]

What about the sense of reality? What role did it play? Segal regarded the gradual giving way of omnipotent thinking to more realistic thinking as crucial to a growing acknowledgment of difference between ego and object and hence to symbol formation. In this fashion, without dotting the *i*'s and crossing the *t*'s, she made a sense of reality a necessary condition for creating and using symbols. Simultaneously she embedded the development of reality thinking in a narrative of loving and hating. It was left to Bion to set that thinking free and secure it an independent status.

*   *   *

Bion like Segal worked with psychotics. Like Segal too, he was concerned with their reality thinking or rather lack thereof. Both also focused on the ego; but of its dual meanings – ego as self and ego as some sort of psychical agency – they chose a different one to emphasize. (Klein, like Freud, but more so, slid between the two.) Segal, in writing about the ego's confusion with objects, highlighted self; Bion, in exploring the ego as the instrument for thought, stressed agency.

Bion assumed, and made this assumption his point of departure, that the psychotic, or rather the person who became psychotic, was inordinately endowed with destructive impulses, aimed, above all, at reality, external and internal alike. This hatred extended to all that made awareness of reality possible – including his or her mental apparatus:

As a result of these . . . attacks . . . those features of the personality which should one day provide the foundation for intuitive under-standing of himself and others are jeopardized at the outset. . . . [T]he functions which Freud described as being, at a later stage, a develop-mental response to the reality principle, that is to say, consciousness of sense impressions, attention, memory, judgement, thought, have brought against them, in such inchoate form as they may possess at the outset of life, the sadistic splitting eviscerating attacks that lead to their being minutely fragmented and then expelled from the personality.

Not surprisingly the psyche of the psychotic came to be seriously depleted. At the same time his or her world became more and more menacing – thanks to the accumulation of ejected fragments or particles:

> In the patient's phantasy the expelled particles of ego lead an independent and uncontrolled existence, either contained by or containing the external objects; they continue to exercise their functions as if the ordeal to which they have been subjected had served only to increase their number and provoke their hostility to the psyche that ejected them. In consequence the patient feels himself to be surrounded by bizarre objects.[35]

Bion was trying to investigate phenomena that suggested a crippling of the patient's capacity for thought. Nowhere did he provide a more vivid description than in his paper "On Hallucination" (1958). In it he reported on sessions from an analysis of a certified schizophrenic, an analysis that had been underway "for some years" and in which a great deal of work "had already been done." Here is the first of those sessions:

> The patient has arrived on time and I have asked him to be called. . . . As he passes into the room he glances rapidly at me; such frank scrutiny has been a development of the past six months and is still a novelty. While I close the door he goes to the foot of the couch, facing the head pillows and my chair, and stands, shoulders stooping, knees sagging, head inclined to the chair, motionless until I have passed him and am about to sit down. So closely do his movements seem to be geared with mine that the inception of my movements to sit appear to release a spring in him. As I lower myself into my seat he turns left about, slowly, evenly, as if something would be spilled, or perhaps fractured, were he to be betrayed into a precipitate movement. As I sit the turning movement stops as if we were both parts of the same clockwork toy. The patient, now with his back to me, is arrested at a moment when his gaze is directed to the floor near the corner of the room which would be to his right and facing him if he lay on the couch. The pause endures perhaps a second and is closed by a shudder of his head and shoulders which is so slight and so rapid that I might suppose myself mistaken. Yet it marks the end of one phase and the start of the next; the patient seats himself on the couch preparatory to lying down.
> He reclines slowly, keeping his eyes on the corner of the floor, craning his head forward now and then as he falls back on the couch as if anxious not to become unsighted. His scrutiny, as if he feared the consequences of being detected in it, is circumspect.
> He is recumbent at last: a few more surreptitious glances and he is still. Then he speaks: "I feel quite empty. Although I have hardly eaten

anything, it can't be that. No, it's no use; I shan't be able to do any more today." He then relapses into silence.

Watching these opening moves, Bion recalled how the previous day's session had ended. The patient had been "hostile and afraid that he would murder" his analyst. Bion had interpreted his patient's splitting off "painful feelings, mostly envy and revenge," forcing them into his analyst, and so getting rid of them. (Had killing his analyst – in whom his own envy and revenge had been lodged – seemed, to the patient, the surest way to protect himself? Bion did not say.) What Bion had now witnessed he saw as an effort by the patient "to remove" from his analyst "those bad aspects of himself before he attempted the main business of the session, the ingestion of cure."

> When the patient glanced at me he was taking a part of me into him. It was taken into his eyes, . . . as if his eyes could suck something out of me. This was then removed from me, before I sat down, and expelled, again through his eyes, so that it was deposited in the right-hand corner of the room where he could keep it under observation while he was lying on the couch. The expulsion took a moment or two. . . . The shudder I have described was the sign that the expulsion was complete. . . .
>
> To turn now to the object supposedly deposited in the corner of the room. . . . Evidently it is an hostile object: its extrusion has emptied the patient: its presence threatens him and makes him fear he will be able to make no further use of the session.

Most of these reflections Bion apparently communicated to his patient, all the while observing him carefully:

> [The patient] made jerky convulsive movements which were confined mostly to the upper part of his body. Every syllable I uttered seemed to be felt by him as a stabbing thrust from me. I pointed this out and said that he felt a very bad thing was being violently intruded into him, partly by me, and partly by himself in spite of the precaution he had taken by hardly eating anything. . . . The convulsive movements stopped.

The session continued in such a fashion as to prompt Bion to draw his patient's attention to an aspect of the analytic situation itself:

> It is that the patient is . . . expressing, with an unusual degree of urgency and force, a belief in his capacity to communicate matters, which he feels to be worth while, to a person whom he thinks likely to be receptive to them.

This hour ranked, for analyst and patient alike, as a good one. Sessions of this sort, Bion had noticed, "were followed with great consistency by 'bad'" ones in which "the patient seemed to return to an . . . uncooperative state of mind and produced material" that Bion "found almost impossible to interpret." The next one ran true to form:

> The patient came in, gave me [Bion] a swift glance, waited till I reached my chair, and then lay down without further ado. He said tonelessly: "I don't know how much I shall be able to do today." . . . At this point I felt his attention began to wander and he faltered in his speech. . . . He went on: "I am definitely anxious. Slightly. Still I suppose it does not matter." . . . [H]e continued, "I asked for some coffee. She seemed upset. It may have been my voice but it was definitely good coffee too. I don't know why I shouldn't like it. When I passed the mews I thought the walls bulged outwards. I went back later but it was all right." There was more that I cannot attempt to reconstruct.

The patient's associations became less, rather than more, coherent:

> [They] seemed to consist of parts of sentences, disjointed references to what I assumed to be actual events, and a certain amount of material which had meaning for me because it had appeared in other sessions. . . . [T]he session came to an end without my being able to formulate any clear idea of what was going on. I said that we did not know why all his analytic intuition and understanding had disappeared. He said "Yes" commiseratingly, and if one word can be made to express "and I think that your intuition must have gone too," then his "Yes" did so on this occasion.[36]

Having got rid of things, including his capacity for judgment, how might Bion's patient take them back and retain them? Or to put it another way: if working through attacks on the ego figured as crucial, how did Bion conceptualize its happening? He did not address this question explicitly in his paper on hallucinations. Elsewhere he wrote of projective identification in reverse. During treatment, he claimed, the patient attempts to bring back "expelled particles of ego and their accretions," by the same route by which they had been expelled. But according to Bion's own reckoning, such attempts were likely to fail. How could it be otherwise? The objects expelled by projective identification became "infinitely worse after expulsion" than they had been when originally expelled. Consequently the patient felt "intruded upon, assaulted, and tortured by this re-entry even if willed by himself."[37] As an account of reconstituting the ego, projective identification in reverse came up short.

*   *   *

Bion did not abandon this concept. Instead he extended and elaborated it. He began by taking a cue from Klein. She had written of the ego's excessive projective identification and "expelling into the outer world parts of itself" and how, as a consequence, the ego was deprived of "desired qualities" such as "power, potency, strength, knowledge," all of which were bound up with the less desirable "aggressive component of feelings."[38] Excessive compared to what? To an amount or kind of projective identification that might be regarded as normal? Implicit in Klein's comment was a notion of projective identification as nonpathological. Bion adopted this suggestion and simply declared: "I shall suppose that there is a normal degree of projective identification, without defining the limits within which normality lies."[39]

For both Klein and Bion "normal" carried with it the connotation of developmental. Where Klein wrote of the development of the ego through repeated cycles of projection and introjection, Bion took it further in claiming that these were cycles of projective and introjective identification. A claim about development which, Bion acknowledged, rested on work with an (unspecified) adult analysand:

> When the patient strove to rid himself of fears of death which were felt to be too powerful for his personality to contain he split off his fears and put them into me, the idea apparently being that if they were allowed to repose there long enough they would undergo modification by my psyche and could be safely reintrojected. On the occasion that I have in mind the patient had felt . . . that I evacuated them so quickly that the feelings were not modified, but had become more painful. . . .
>
> [W]hat he felt was my refusal to accept parts of his personality. Consequently he strove to force them into me with increased desperation and violence. His behaviour, isolated from the context of the analysis, might have appeared to be an expression of primary aggression. The more violent his phantasies of projective identification, the more frightened he became of me. . . . The analytic situation built up in my mind a sense of witnessing an extremely early scene. I felt that the patient had experienced in infancy a mother who dutifully responded to the infant's emotional displays. The dutiful response had in it an element of impatient "I don't know what's the matter with the child." My deduction was that in order to understand what the child wanted the mother should have treated the infant's cry as more than a demand for her presence. From the infant's point of view she should have taken into her, and thus experienced, the fear that the child was dying. It was this fear that the child could not contain. He strove to split it off together with the part of his personality in which it lay and to project it into the

mother. An understanding mother is able to experience the feeling of dread, that her baby is striving to deal with by projective identification, and yet retain a balanced outlook. This patient had had to deal with a mother who could not tolerate experiencing such feelings and reacted either by denying them ingress, or alternatively by becoming a prey to the anxiety which resulted from the introjection of the infant's feelings. The latter reaction must, I think, have been rare: denial was dominant.[40]

Note two moves Bion made in this passage. First, he shifted from an imagined infant to an imagined mother. Second, he slid from nature to nurture, from the infant's innate death instinct and inordinate destructive impulses to the mother's capacity for containing projective identifications or her capacity for reverie – the state of mind the infant required of the mother if she were to take in the infant's feelings and make them seem bearable. Bion's mother as container derived from the external world: she closely resembled a mother who might actually have been available very early in life.

Then Bion added another dimension: he introduced a need to know. Where Freud spoke of sexual curiosity, Klein of the epistemophilic impulse, Bion wrote of a thirst "to understand, comprehend the reality of, get insight into the nature of . . . oneself or another." Where Freud and Klein had put the spotlight on the infant, Bion brought the mother as container into the picture. He described the link between her mind and its contents as being of three kinds: "L," "H," and "K," standing for loving, hating, and wanting to know. "Mother" at times loved her infant, hated him, or found herself trying to understand how he was experiencing, feeling, thinking; her linking with her infant in this third way allowed him to introject an understanding object and, in turn, promoted his capacity for thought. Bion thus implicitly rejected theories that viewed "thinking as merely the emergence or maturation of an autonomous ego function." According to him, K was "hard-won by the infant ego from emotional experiences with a nurturing object, functioning normally on the reality principle."[41]

*   *   *

Bion said relatively little about guilt. (In comparison, Segal wrote a good deal: she echoed Klein's distinction between persecutory and depressive anxiety; she also adopted Klein's notions of reparation and the depressive position.) But his conceptualization of the K link proved fruitful in two ways that complemented each other. In the first instance his work prompted a fresh look at the resources available to the ego in its struggle with the superego and/or internal objects. In the second instance his ideas implied that the key to a shift in the balance of power between them lay in the domain of knowledge and judgment. Both Joseph and Britton exploited these suggestions.

The ego gaining ground

"Enlarging the ego" – enabling "the personality to contain and be responsible for more aspects of itself" – this Joseph considered central to the therapeutic enterprise.[42] She echoed Bion's emphasis on an understanding object, yet refrained from speculating about infancy, from constructing a story of "in the beginning"; instead she offered observations gleaned from the here and now of the analytic treatment. Britton, roughly two decades Joseph's junior – Joseph was born in 1917 – addressed more specifically the ego's subordination to the superego – to a superego, as Freud put it, "turned against the ego, . . . a pure culture of the death instinct."[43] How to modify this potentially "ego-destructive superego"?[44] In Klein's account love figured as absolutely necessary: discovering one's love for this hostile object allowed, indeed prompted, a reassessment of its fearfulness. Britton, following Bion, claimed that a dose of reality was equally necessary. The issue, in his mind, was not simply one of reappraising the superego but of disempowering it and thus emancipating oneself from something deadly.

*   *   *

"Enlarging the ego" presupposed the analyst's being able to make contact with the patient – a presupposition that, Joseph noted, frequently proved unwarranted. She was intrigued by patients whom she referred to as being "difficult to reach," by which she meant difficult to reach with interpretations and thereby "to give them real emotional understanding."

> In psychoanalytic discussions on technique, stress has frequently been laid on the importance of a working or therapeutic alliance between analyst and patient. What impresses one early in the treatment of this group of unreachable patients is that what looks like a therapeutic alliance turns out to be inimical to a real alliance, and that what is termed understanding is actually anti-understanding. Many of these patients tend to respond quickly to interpretations, using such expressions as "do you mean," referring to previous dreams and the like and seeming eminently cooperative and helpful. One finds oneself in a situation that looks exactly like an on-going analysis with understanding, . . . appreciation, and even reported improvement. And yet one has a feeling of hollowness.

Her countertransference led Joseph to be wary: "it may seem all a bit too easy, pleasant, and unconflicted, or signs of conflict may emerge but are somehow quickly dissipated."

> In the treatment of such cases I believe we can observe a splitting within the personality, so that one part of the ego is kept at a distance

from the analyst and the analytic work. Sometimes this is difficult to see since the patient may appear to be working and cooperating with the analyst, but the part of the personality that is available is actually keeping another more needy or potentially responsive and receptive part split off. Sometimes the split takes the form of one part of the ego standing aside as if observing all that is going on between the analyst and the other part of the patient and destructively preventing real contact being made, using various methods of avoidance and evasion. Sometimes large parts of the ego temporarily seem to disappear in the analysis with resultant apathy or extreme passivity – often associated with the powerful use of projective identification.[45]

Joseph expanded. In "The Patient Who Is Difficult to Reach" (1975), she reported on an analysand she called C.:

C. was at this time feeling insecure about the progress of the treatment, being very much aware of its length and feeling rather hopeless and impotent. This type of depression and open anxiety was unusual. During a session he was able to understand a point that I was making. Then he realized that although the understanding seemed helpful to him, he had become quiet. I commented on the feeling of his having made a sudden shift to passivity. C. then started to speak, and explained that he felt "pulled inside" and as if I would now expect him to speak, to "perform," and he felt he could not. I was then able to show him that he had felt understood, but this experience of being understood was concretely experienced as if he were being drawn into the understanding, as into my inside, and then frightened that I was going to expect him to pull outside and to talk, "to perform."

Subsequently he added that he felt as if he were in a box lying on his side looking outwards, but into the darkness. The box was closed round him. After a few minutes he started to talk about "something else." At a dinner party the other night he had met a woman colleague. She was wearing a very lovely dress; he had congratulated her on it; it had three, horizontal eye-shaped slits near the top – if only he had had three eyes and could have looked out of all three at once. It was almost the end of the session, and I commented that what he wanted now was to get completely inside me through the slits with his eyes, with his whole self, totally inside me and remain there, as in the box. I also added that from the way he spoke he was conveying a very urgent need to make me aware of the importance of his desire to be shut away inside.

When he arrived the following day he commented that the end of the previous session had touched him deeply, but afterwards he had felt as though I had caught him in some guilty secret. I suggested that he had experienced my interpretation of this intense desire to be inside via the slits in the dress, as actually encouraging him to project himself into my inside, and that "understanding" had then been experienced as my doing something exciting and illicit with him. . . . So one could follow the movement of the session from the real understanding and direct contact between analyst and the more responsive parts of the patient to a flight into a concretely experienced inanimate object, which again rendered him passive and withdrawn and largely unable to be reached.

Repeatedly analyst and patient went through "a sequence in which within one session he [the patient] made progress, became deeply involved and moved by what was going on, but the following day it was a mere flat memory." Repeatedly Joseph saw her patient retreat to a familiar and well-established position that allowed the emotional self to remain unavailable while "a weakly pseudo-cooperative part" carried on a conversation with her.[46]

C. reappeared – now called N. – in "Psychic Change and the Psycho-analytic Process" (1989). Joseph brought material from his analysis when termination was under discussion, material that was "deeply influenced" by the prospect of ending treatment: "this was . . . bringing up a great need to protest, to go backwards and mobilize old defensive retreats." And "though far from perfect, in view of the nature of the patient, . . . the result of treatment . . . seemed quite encouraging. . . . He had come as a very schizoid, passive man, who, . . . now, was happily married, positively enjoying life and much more thoughtful and concerned as a human being."

The session was a Friday. My patient, N., arrived saying that he felt bad and anxious, as if too much was going on. He and his wife were currently selling their house and there were important changes going on in his work. I clarified that it seemed that the anxiety was more focused round the issue of stopping the analysis. This he agreed but went on to describe in detail his feelings of discomfort as if he was angry and resentful. I thought at that point, and suggested that it was partly that he had not really been able to believe that I could let him go, but that now he was having to face this aspect of stopping. (This patient had for a very long time lived in the belief that he was the very special child of his mother, he was in fact the youngest of the family; and he believed that he was my very special patient, and from this angle alone the idea of stopping treatment had been very difficult to accept.)

My patient responded, however, to my remark by going back to discussing his difficulties, his resentment, his coldness, and so on. I thought, and showed him, that he was sinking into a kind of anger and misery – shown by his settling into and stressing all the difficulties and getting caught up into it, in order to avoid the specific feelings about actually leaving and what it really meant to him at that moment. In other words, I thought he was sinking into a kind of bog of misery as a defence, so that the anger was part of the bog and was not anger in its own right.

N. became silent – a pause – and then said he had the thought "clever old bag." He explained he thought I was right and that he was aware that when he made the remark that he resented my being right, so he went quiet. Now we could both agree about the misery, being used actively as a kind of masochistic defence, and he himself had clear insight into his resentment about my being right.

N. went on to talk about this and how, when I had first spoken about the defensiveness and he went quiet, he felt he was taking over what I was saying and, as he put it, "putting it into a box." I discussed with him the way he had not quite been able to acknowledge that I was right – and that he was grateful and how this very awareness stimulated rivalry and envy. Clearly, by now his mood had changed and he was talking freely. N. went on to say that he had now gone off at a tangent. He was thinking about yesterday. They had been invited by the Xes where the wife is a very poor cook, so his wife had a brilliant idea. She would offer to make a summer pudding, which the patient just adores, and they would take it with them to the supper. He would help his wife by topping and tailing the fruit. This was said in a very positive and warm way.

Here it was clear that N. was describing a movement, that he had now got into contact with a good experience again, with a feeling that there was a good smell and a good taste about, and appreciation of what I had been able to see and what he really deeply knew about the analysis. Also there was awareness that he could help to get hold of these feelings and get the analysis consolidated, as is shown by his telling about helping his wife preparing the fruit. . . .

[T]owards the end of the session N. talked about a feeling that he had had about analysis, how he thought that not only he, but he believed, I, the analyst, must have some special feelings about his leaving and about our work together. I think that we can see the shift in my patient's feelings during the session. At the beginning he was largely sinking into a bog of mindless misery, by the end he was well in contact with very moving feelings of loss and contact with myself.[47]

Something that looked like "enlarging the ego" was underway. As to how this enlargement came about, Joseph gave no schematic answer. One can, however, tease out of her writings a twofold reply. The first piece hinges on the patient's retrieving projections. In line with Bion, Joseph appreciated that it was one thing, by paying close attention to what was being lived – or acted – in the transference-countertransference situation, to grasp the meaning of the patient's projected fragments and quite another for the patient to take back the projections into himself.

> With . . . [a female] patient it was possible to open up her feelings that I was antagonistic and controlling, that I did not want her to get on in her life or in her career. As we looked at her feelings about my motivation it became clear that in her mind I felt threatened by her, and deeply envious of her as a young intelligent person with her life ahead of her. I would then wish to explore more carefully her picture of me, this old, supposedly lonely, rather embittered person, . . . and only very slowly and over a long period, hope to explore how much of these thoughts might be linked with actual observations of myself . . ., how much projected parts of herself. . . . To assume that all these ideas were projections from the beginning would almost certainly be inaccurate, would numb one's sensitivity . . . to what was going on and prevent one from seeing what else was being talked about and why it came up at that moment.

This slow and tactful exploration, this careful and consistent effort to show the patient how and why he was again and again splitting off part of his self – which was in large measure "what we mean when we talk about 'containing'" – aimed to foster ego integration.[48] The second piece hinges on the patient's "comfortable identification with the analyst and the analytic process." Where Bion spoke of the introjection of an understanding object as crucial for ego functioning, more particularly, for the capacity to think and to learn from experience, Joseph suggested that identification with the analyst and the analytic process was crucial for strengthening that part of the patient's ego that was able "moment to moment . . . to investigate" what was "going on inside himself" and "to take responsibility for . . . [his] own insight."[49] As she saw it, ego integration and ego strengthening went hand in hand – and made possible collaboration, albeit intermittent, between analyst and patient.

*   *   *

Disempowering the superego[50] – this was the internal drama that Britton addressed in his chapter "Emancipation from the Superego." He began by reminding his readers of James Strachey's 1934 paper and his claim that the therapeutic effect of analysis resulted from a mellowing of the superego:

> His [Strachey's] idea was based on Melanie Klein's description of the cycle of projection and re-introjection. He suggested that a severe superego can be modified within the transference by . . . re-introjection

... of projections onto the analyst [that have been] modified by ... the patient's experience of the analyst.[51]

Britton wanted to supplement Strachey's emphasis on the character of the superego: he wanted to direct attention to the relationship of the ego to the superego. He drew a political analogy:

> In a monarchic autocracy, the character of the monarch is likely to vary from one ruler to another, with considerable consequences for the subjects. Modifying the character of the autocrat is of great significance therefore, and so it is in the internal world. However, permanent improvement in the well-being of the citizens of the state depends on modifying the constitutional relationship between the crown and the commonwealth. Similarly, in the internal world the position of the ego in relation to the occupant of the seat of conscience is crucial. Even when the superego retains its adverse character, analysis can help the ... ego ... wrest from the superego the function of judging both internal and external reality. This I think of as the ego's *emancipation*.[52]

For material to illustrate his argument, to catch the high drama of a duel between ego and superego, Britton turned to the Book of Job. He assigned the role of ego to Job, and then, following Freud's lead – Freud had understood God to be the external representation of the superego – he assigned God the part of superego. (Britton also followed the lead given by Jack Miles in his "postmodern account." It made, Britton claimed, the "most sense.")[53]

The story itself starts with a wager between God and Satan, that is, God praises Job as "a blameless and upright man who fears God and turns away from evil" and Satan counters that his virtues are contingent upon his good fortune. Take away that good fortune, Satan says to God, "stretch out your hand now, and touch all that he has, and he will curse you to your face."[54] God accepts the challenge and allows Satan to set to work. As part of the gamble, Satan is permitted to slay all of Job's sons, daughters, and servants. Job does not curse God, and God thinks that he has won the bet. But no, Satan insists on continuing the contest:

> "Skin for skin! All that people have they will give to save their lives. But stretch out your hand and touch his bone and flesh, and he will curse you to your face." The LORD said to Satan, "Very well, he is in your power; only spare his life." So Satan went out from the presence of the LORD, and inflicted loathsome sores on Job from the sole of his foot to the crown of his head. Job took a potsherd to scrape himself, and sat among the ashes.[55]

Still Job does not curse God. Nor is he contrite. He is neither persuaded by those who imply that he must have done something wrong and that, to defend himself against God, he must be spotless and above reproach, nor is he convinced by those who assert that God needs no justification. In all his pain and grief, he insists on his own righteousness and demands that God explain why he must suffer. The stage is thus set for a confrontation between God and Job.

Few speeches can more properly be called overpowering than the Lord's to Job from the whirlwind (*Job* 38–41). He tells nothing of himself, he tells solely of his power. Might makes right, he bellows at Job. "Only if and when the wretch scraping his sores with a potsherd can unleash a demonstration of power comparable to the Lord's own will the Lord take the wretch's objections seriously."[56]

> "Deck yourself with majesty and dignity;
> clothe yourself with glory and splendor.
> Pour out the overflowings of your anger,
> and look on all who are proud and abuse them.
> Look on all who are proud and bring them low;
> tread down the wicked where they stand.
> Hide them all in the dust together;
> bind their faces in the world below.
> Then I will also acknowledge to you
> that your own right hand can give you victory."[57]

God thus presents himself, "with withering sarcasm and towering bravado, as an . . . irresistible force"; about his justice, he says nothing. How could he? "He has subjected a just man to torture on a whim. The question then becomes, as the creature lies naked in his agony, listening to his creator boast of his power to tame whales: *Will Job be taken in*?"[58]

Job's response is concise – seven verses in two short statements, in answer to 123 verses from God. Here is Job's first reply:

> "See, I am of small account; what shall I answer you?
> I lay my hand on my mouth.
> I have spoken once, and I will not answer;
> twice, but will proceed no further."[59]

"So much and no more. Job concedes nothing." "What shall I answer you?" amounts to an evasion. "I am of small account" echoes what Job has said all along. "I have spoken once, and will not answer; twice, but will proceed no further" defies "the thunderer's demand that Job comment on his thunder."[60] Job thus says just enough to let his audience know that he is acknowledging God's power, but going no farther: he is not being taken in.

About Job's first reply, there is little exegetical dispute. Not so with the second. The last two lines – the linchpin of the traditional interpretation of Job's speech as an outright recantation – read:

> "therefore I despise myself,
> and repent in dust and ashes."[61]

Miles questioned the translation, particularly the word "myself." "No word," he claimed, "has less support from the original" than this one. He continued with the phrase "dust and ashes." Reading it "as a reference to mankind in its mortal frailty, reading the verbs that the [N]RSV translates 'despise myself and repent' as transitive, with 'dust and ashes' or (more idiomatically) 'mortal man' as their common object," he translated the closing words: "I shudder with sorrow for mortal clay." In short, Job holds out to the very end: he refuses to accept mere physical force as the criterion of moral integrity.[62]

This interpretation of Job as intransigent served Britton well:

> Taking it to be the ego and superego in the story, it [Job's reply to God] represents a crucial moment in development when the ego takes the superego to task and, while still afraid of its power, claims the right to question its judgement and to doubt its motives. This is, I think, also a crucial moment in some analyses when the individual can question the authenticity of the voice of adverse judgement, whether it is experienced as coming from within as self-condemnation or by projection as coming from the analyst.

Writing of a female patient, Britton elaborated:

> Repeatedly disentangling what belonged to her and what was a property of her object was crucial. . . . The overall effect was that the internal object – which could only be described as murderous – lost its moral power within the patient's internal polity and could no longer be described as having the role of conscience, with its claim of moral judgement.

All the same, this "gradual displacement" of the hostile superego and/or internal object "from its position of moral arbiter" was no easy matter.[63]

This very difficulty caused Britton to flinch. He asked: Does a harsh, "forbidding superego" afflict only "some unfortunate individuals?" It was his "impression that it figures in the personality of particular people in whom it produces a particular severity and rigidity." He seemed ready to draw a sharp line between normal and abnormal forms of the superego.[64] He seemed equally ready to ignore what Freud had written about such a distinction, albeit with regard to the ego: "[A] normal ego . . . is, like normality in general, an ideal fiction. . . . Every normal person, in fact, is only normal on the average."[65] Change ego to superego, that is, a normal superego is an ideal fiction. The result: a sobering assessment of psychic reality.

*   *   *

Recall that Chapters 2 and 3 ended with omnipotence of thought holding sway and figuring as crucial to complex defensive systems – thanks to which a person warded off or evaded unbearable guilt. The centrality of such thinking led me to claim that questions of moral and cognitive development were deeply entwined. At this point it may be helpful to review the innovations discussed in this chapter – innovations that made the ego, rather than the superego, the site of moral judgment.

I began the chapter with Klein's emphasis on unconscious fantasy, with the heat her position generated during the Controversial Discussions of the 1940s. Susan Isaacs, deputed to speak for the Kleinians, thought of fantasy as "the mental corollary, the psychic representative of instinct." There was "no impulse, no instinctual urge or response," she wrote, that was "not experienced as (unconscious) phantasy."[66] This claim fueled suspicions on both sides of the Atlantic that "unconscious phantasies were . . . interpreted to the patient immediately and very directly in part-object language (breast, nipple, penis etc.)."[67] The Kleinians were seen, and presented themselves, as rushing straight to the depths, with scant regard for either their patients' external reality or their ego functioning.

Fast forward to 40 plus years after the Controversial Discussions, to the work of Betty Joseph, a leading contemporary Kleinian. In writing about "unreachable patients," in depicting her efforts to make more of the ego available, Joseph paid close attention to "the patient's method of communication," the actual way he spoke, and the way he reacted to her interpretations. And she urged other analysts to do likewise: "to recognize that these patients, even when . . . quite verbal," were "in fact doing a great deal of acting sometimes in speech itself."[68] More generally, she urged her colleagues to concentrate on the detailed interaction of the session, to describe fully how the patient is using the analyst, using interpretations, and using his mind, in short, to concentrate on phenomena immediately accessible to the patient – and then move to the analysis of the way the patient's history and unconscious fantasies express themselves in the session.[69] What accounts for the sea-change that occurred in those intervening four decades?

Already in 1943 Klein expressed her concern that Isaacs had gone too far, that she, Klein, "could not agree to the concept of unconscious phantasy being . . . everything to begin with on the mental side."[70] As she saw it, the reality principle as well as pleasure principle operated from birth onward. Both Segal and Bion pursued the question of reality thinking and took up matters of ego functioning. Segal's was the more cautious approach: she argued that the cognitive issues of concern to her – principally symbol formation – could be subsumed under Klein's concepts of the paranoid-schizoid and depressive positions. Bion's was the more radical: he stretched and re-fashioned the notion of projective identification to produce an object-relations story of cognitive development or, as he put it, of forging the K link. And though Kleinians did not and still do not "draw systematic distinctions between self concepts and ego concepts [–] . . . they speak comfortably about attacks on the ego, the self, even the mind, in a way that refers in part to actual functional disturbances and in part to unconscious fantasies of the ego, self, or mind being a substance that can be ejected, spoiled, or broken into pieces"[71] – Bion, and following his lead, Joseph and Britton, gave ego functioning a prominence that Klein had rarely bestowed on it.

This brings me to my final point: that an analyst may entertain hopes for the enlargement of her patient's ego and a corresponding disempowerment of an ego-destructive superego, speaks to her confidence in her patient – not only as a potentially reasonable person, but as a moral one as well.

Extracts from *Second Thoughts* by W. R. Bion by permission of Paterson Marsh Ltd on behalf of the Estate of W. R. Bion.

Conclusion

With the introduction of the superego, as I said at the outset, Freud made clear that he regarded the study of moral development as central to psychoanalytic theory. At the same time he based that study on a reconception of guilt: he thought of it not only as conscious, but as unconscious as well, and it was the unconscious sense of guilt that became a concern peculiar to the discipline he was founding.[1] Just how peculiar, Freud may not have fully appreciated. Melanie Klein was of the opinion that "after F[reud] had discovered the super-ego and the unc. feeling of guilt he had not added to . . . [these] discoveries." As she saw it, "the super-ego was a new beginning towards the understanding of the unc. and of internal relationships as they have never been understood apart from poets."[2]

In this book I have not focused strictly on the superego. I have fitted it into a larger psychoanalytic narrative of guilt and its vicissitudes. At this point it may be helpful to review that narrative, and to do so as a series of moves that successively deepened the explanation of moral development and gave it an increasingly psychoanalytic character.

*   *   *

I also indicated that Freud and Klein's was a naturalistic approach. A moral sense, they both presumed, was natural, but not native. They thought of it, I suggested, as an emergent phenomenon. So they interested themselves in its history – and offered various scenarios. Let me start with the different varieties.

In Freud's standard account, the superego figures as heir to the Oedipus complex: When, in the male child, the "complete Oedipus complex" (positive and negative) is "demolished," the boy gives up his attachments to his mother and father and instead identifies with these parental figures.[3] (Identification is a slippery concept. Elsewhere Freud spoke of "the introjection of the object into the ego" or "the shadow of the object falling on the ego.")[4] In the context of the vanishing Oedipus complex, the identifications produce a permanent differentiation within the ego: this "*modification of the ego retains its special position; it confronts the other contents of the ego as . . . [a] super-ego.*"[5] As for what might be called Klein's standard version, it amounted to a major revision. In the late 1920s she expressed her skepticism about the superego being deposited as the Oedipus complex dissolved and recommended two qualifications: the superego is formed in tandem with oedipal experiences, and it has already undergone extraordinary vicissitudes before the oedipal phase draws to a close. Klein never did discard the Oedipus complex: in the 1930s she tried to unite it with the depressive position. But in linking the two, she gave the depressive position pride of place.

Having paid scant attention to Freud's ontogenetic story, I emphasized his much ridiculed phylogenetic tale. Human beings, he wrote, adopting a hypothesis from Darwin, lived together in the prehistoric past in small hordes, each consisting of several adult females and their offspring and ruled over by a terrible and violent adult male. The violent male, father of the offspring, had driven off every other adult male and had thus banished every challenger to his monopoly on sexual relations with the horde's females. Freud then further speculated that the male offspring grew up loving and admiring the ruler, their father, but hating and fearing him as well. These young males, having reached adulthood and having been expelled from the horde, acted on their shared wish to be rid of their father: they banded together, returned, and slew him. Afterward their love for the dead man resurfaced, and they experienced guilt and remorse. (In expiation thereof they set up their father, in the guise of a totem, as a deity and instituted prohibitions against killing and incest.) Even after Freud worked out his concept of the superego, he insisted, as he had done in *Totem and Taboo*, that "the conflict arising from ambivalence – the conflict between . . . two primal instincts – leaves . . . behind . . . a sense of guilt."[6]

By a different route Klein arrived at the centrality of ambivalence and found herself, like Freud, ready to claim that the "*affectionate* current of feeling" creates genuine moral sensibilities.[7] Her journey proceeded in four stages. The first has been alluded to already: Klein's reframing of the Oedipus complex and the superego, more particularly, her early dating of their joint appearance. In contrast to Freud, and here she took a second step, she maintained that "from the beginning of post-natal life . . . the infant has a relation to the mother (although focusing primarily on her breast) which is imbued with . . . love, hatred, phantasies, anxieties, and defences."[8] Then a third step: the object relation that comes into being at birth is not simply a relation to an external object. Introjection and projection also start with the first feeding:

[These] processes . . . lead to the institution inside ourselves of loved and hated objects, who are felt to be "good" and "bad," and who are interrelated with each other and with the self: that is to say, they constitute . . . a complex object world, which is felt by the individual, in deep layers of the unconscious, to be concretely inside himself, and for which I and my colleagues therefore use the term "internalized objects" and an "inner world."[9]

Finally – and fourth – to the depressive position: the infant, so Klein claimed, passes from a part-object relation to a relation with a whole object. At this point the loved and loving object – the good object – comes into its own. The infant becomes dependent upon it and its internalized counterpart with a new force. The infant also becomes full of anxiety – anxiety that the vehemence of his feelings, his love as well as his hate, may imperil his good object. And not only anxiety: guilt and remorse are its constant companions.

I want to highlight here a discrepancy between Freud's ontogenetic account of moral development and Klein's formulation of the depressive position. Freud's rendering lays itself open to a sociological construal of guilt. In *Civilization and Its Discontents*, for example, he wrote:

> At the beginning . . . what is bad is whatever causes one to be threat-
> ened with loss of love. . . . [A]t this stage the sense of guilt is clearly
> only a fear of loss of love, "social" anxiety. In small children it can
> never be anything else, but in many adults, too, it has only changed to
> the extent that the place of the father or the two parents is taken by the
> larger human community. Consequently, such people habitually allow
> themselves to do any bad thing which promises them enjoyment, so
> long as they are sure that the authority will not know anything about it
> or cannot blame them for it; they are afraid only of being found out.[10]

In contrast, Klein's is a more consistently psychological or intrapsychic understanding. Both regarded guilt as an emergent phenomenon, but where Freud might consider a young child amoral, Klein saw him as already a moral agent or at least a proto-moral one.

Klein soon expanded her developmental narrative to include that proto-moral being. As she put it, "in the course of working out" her "concept of the infantile depressive position, . . . the problems of the phase preceding it again forced themselves" on her attention.[11] Indeed she was returning to themes explored earlier; in the 1920s she had grappled with sadism and the punitive superego – a cruel internal object – that it engendered. (She and her followers have tended to use the concepts of superego and internal objects interchangeably.) With her formulation of the paranoid-schizoid position, Klein postulated a distinction between persecutory and depressive anxiety – between concern for the self and concern for the other. (Contemporary Kleinians have faithfully reiterated this distinction.) All the same, Klein appreciated its artificial character. Since some internalization of the object, she argued, is bound to occur, anxiety on behalf of the object is bound to be mixed with anxiety on behalf of the ego. She thus continued steadfast in maintaining the fatal inevitability of guilt.

Klein's steadfastness forced subsequent generations of psychoanalysts to ask why guilt is so frequently difficult to detect. How is it evaded, warded off, defended against? In other words, her steadfastness shifted the focus from a developmental tale to problems that practitioners confront in their consulting rooms. In so doing she defined a research – and therapeutic – project that is distinctively psychoanalytic.

*　　*　　*

In the mid-1930s, Joan Riviere wrote what her fellow Kleinians regarded as a seminal paper on a complex defensive organization – the manic defense. According to her, the essential feature of the "manic attitude" is a "*denial of psychical reality*," more particularly, a denial of "the ego's object-relations and its *dependence on its objects*." Along with this goes both "*contempt* and depreciation of the value of . . . objects" and "attempts at inordinate and tyrannical *control and mastery*" of them. With her "refractory patients," she found that their very "inaccessibility is one form of their *denial*; implicitly they deny the value of everything we say. They literally do not allow us to do anything with them, and in the sense of co-operation they do nothing with us. *They* control the analysis, whether or not they do it openly."

Above all, she argued, a manic system served as a "disguise to conceal . . . a more or less depressive condition in the patient." Analysis, if successful, would mean unmasking "the internal depressive reality"; it would mean "making real, 'realizing,' . . . [the] despair . . . and *sense of failure*." It is not difficult to grasp why the patient would want none of it. Yet, "he knows that no one but an analyst ventures to approach even to the fringes of these problems of his; and so he clings to analysis" despite having little faith in it.[12]

Riviere's discussion followed on the heels of Klein's 1935 paper on manic-depressive states. Following on the heels of Klein's 1946 paper on schizoid mechanisms, successive cohorts of her followers highlighted defenses, elaborated into pathological organizations, against anxieties associated with the paranoid-schizoid position – "anxieties and phantasies about inner destruction and ego-disintegration."[13]

On first glance it would be tempting to picture the resulting internal situation as one in which a healthy, sane, but weak part of the self is in the grip of an aggressive, indeed destructive, part – a terrifying internal object or superego. On closer inspection it turns out that the dependent self as innocent victim held captive by an all-mighty organization and helpless to escape or alter the scene is not the whole story. John Steiner offered a finer grained analysis. He discerned "elements . . . in the needy self which often ask for and accept . . . exploitation."[14] He referred to the relationship as perverse, meaning persistent in error, denoting a turning away from reality and urged a detailed exposure of the system, an unmasking of the collusion and illusion at its core.

Omnipotence figured in both Riviere and Steiner's writings. As they used the term, it chiefly stood in opposition to reality, and they viewed it as the crux of complex defensive organizations. A certain indefiniteness remained, but that indefiniteness did not prevent Kleinians of multiple generations from reaching a similar conclusion: questions of moral and cognitive development are deeply entwined.

*   *   *

For psychoanalysts of all persuasions, James Strachey's 1934 paper stands as a landmark in thinking about "the principles of therapeutics . . . in super-ego terms." As he phrased it – in language that may now sound quaint – the neurotic remains trapped: "exposed to the pressure of a savage id on the one hand and a correspondingly savage super-ego on the other." He remains trapped in what Strachey characterized as a vicious circle. The analyst's task, according to Strachey, consists in breaching this circle:

> If . . . the patient could be made less frightened of his super-ego or introjected object, he would project less terrifying imagos on to the outer object and would therefore have less need to feel hostility towards it; the object which he then introjected would in turn be less savage in its pressure upon id-impulses, which would be able to lose something of their primitive ferocity.

In short, a "*benign* circle would be set up instead of a vicious one." The process hinges on the patient's being able – at a critical moment – to distinguish between an archaic fantasy object and the analyst. The patient's sense of reality serves, perforce, as "an essential but . . . very feeble ally."[15]

Wilfred R. Bion, Betty Joseph, and Ronald Britton, by directing attention to the ego, supplemented Strachey's emphasis on the superego. They all took off from Klein's paper on schizoid mechanisms. Bion showed the way: he stretched and refashioned Klein's notion of projective identification to produce an object-relations story of cognitive development and, at the same time, awarded the K link – a wanting to know – a status equal to that of loving and hating. Joseph focused on the clinical implications of Bion's theorizing: she urged analysts to look for that part of the patient's ego that was able, at least intermittently, to take an interest in understanding. "For long-term . . . change, and for thinking about the ending of an analysis," she regarded "the strengthening of this part of the personality" as crucial.[16]

Here Joseph – and Britton – echoed Freud. The therapeutic intention of psychoanalysis, Freud remarked, is to make the ego stronger, "to make it more independent of the super-ego, to widen its field of perception and enlarge its organization."[17] He, in effect, issued a general directive, but he figured out neither the strategy nor the tactics to mount a successful assault. That task was taken up by his Kleinian heirs. In the course of a protracted and difficult campaign, the superego was transformed into a world of internal objects, the ego was seen as fissionable, and the possibility of structural change came to depend on fathoming the transference-countertransference situation. What has remained constant is the hope that the ego, having reclaimed its right to pass judgment, will exercise that right in a manner that is both fair-minded and compassionate.

Notes

Introduction

1 Freud, *The Ego and the Id* (1923), in *SE* 19: 35–36.
2 Ibid., pp. 36, 48; Freud, "The Economic Problem of Masochism" (1924), in *SE* 19: 167; Freud, "An Autobiographical Study" (1925), in *SE* 20: 59; Freud, *The Question of Lay Analysis: Conversations with an Impartial Person* (1926), in *SE* 20: 223; Freud, *New Introductory Lectures on Psycho-Analysis* (1933), in *SE* 22: 64; Freud, *An Outline of Psycho-Analysis* (1940), in *SE* 23: 205.
3 Freud, *The Ego and the Id*, p. 51.
4 W. R. Bion, "Attacks on Linking" (1959), in W. R. Bion, *Second Thoughts: Selected Papers on Psycho-Analysis* (London: Heinemann, 1967; reprint, London: Karnac, Maresfield Reprints, 1984), p. 108.
5 Roy Schafer, "The Contemporary Kleinians of London," *Psychoanalytic Quarterly* 63 (1994): 426.
6 Anna Freud, "Personal Memories of Ernest Jones" (1979), in *The Writings of Anna Freud*. Vol. 8, *Psychoanalytic Psychology and Normal Development 1970–1980* (New York: International Universities Press, 1981), p. 350.
7 Anna Freud, quoted in a memorandum by Sylvia Payne, April 1940, quoted in Phyllis Grosskurth, *Melanie Klein: Her World and Her Work* (New York: Knopf, 1986), p. 256.
8 Memorandum by Melanie Klein, June 27, 1943, quoted in Grosskurth, *Melanie Klein*, pp. 323–324.
9 Joan Riviere, general introduction to Melanie Klein, Paula Heimann, Susan Isaacs, and Joan Riviere, *Developments in Psycho-Analysis* (London: Hogarth Press, 1952), pp. 10–11.
10 Susan Isaacs, Second Discussion of Scientific Controversies, February 17, 1943, in Pearl King and Riccardo Steiner, eds., *The Freud-Klein Controversies 1941–45* (London: Routledge, 1991), p. 382.
11 Klein to Brierley, June 1942, quoted in Grosskurth, *Melanie Klein*, p. 314.
12 I owe this line of argument to Richard Wollheim, *The Thread of Life* (Cambridge, MA: Harvard University Press, 1984), p. 199.

1 An unconscious sense of guilt

1 Jones to Freud, November 26, 1911, *The Complete Correspondence of Sigmund Freud and Ernest Jones, 1908–1939*. Edited by R. Andrew Paskauskas (Cambridge, MA: Harvard University Press, 1993), pp. 122–123.

2 Ferenczi to Freud, June 23, 1913, *The Correspondence of Sigmund Freud and Sándor Ferenczi*. Vol. 1, *1908–1914*. Edited by Eva Brabant, Ernst Falzeder, and Patrizia Giampieri-Deutsch. Translated by Peter T. Hoffer (Cambridge, MA: Harvard University Press, 1993), p. 494.

3 George W. Stocking, Jr., *After Tylor: British Social Anthropology 1888–1951* (Madison, WI: University of Wisconsin Press, 1995), p. 82. See also H. Stuart Hughes, *Consciousness and Society: The Reorientation of European Social Thought 1890–1930*, rev. edn (New York: Vintage, 1977), p. 145.

4 Freud, "'Civilized' Sexual Morality and Modern Nervous Illness" (1908), in *SE* 9: 194–195.

5 Ibid., pp. 185–186 (emphasis in the original).

6 Freud, "Five Lectures on Psycho-Analysis" (1910), in *SE* 11: 47. On Freud's elaboration of the oedipal etiology of the neuroses, see Judith M. Hughes, *From Freud's Consulting Room: The Unconscious in a Scientific Age* (Cambridge, MA: Harvard University Press, 1994), pp. 70–94.

7 Freud, "Formulations on the Two Principles of Mental Functioning" (1911), in *SE* 12: 225.

8 Freud, *Totem and Taboo: Some Points of Agreement between the Mental Lives of Savages and Neurotics* (1913), in *SE* 13: 86.

9 Ibid., pp. 87, 85.

10 Freud, "Notes upon a Case of Obsessional Neurosis" (1909), in *SE* 10: 187.

11 Ibid., p. 234.

12 Freud, "Two Principles of Mental Functioning," p. 219 (emphasis in the original).

13 Ibid., p. 222 (emphasis in the original).

14 Freud, *Totem and Taboo*, p. 76.

15 Ibid., pp. 79–80. Freud quoted the account of the Egyptian ritual from James G. Frazer, *The Magic Art*, 2 vols. (London, 1911), 1: 67.

16 Freud, *Totem and Taboo*, p. 83.

17 Ibid., pp. 18, 21, 22.

18 Ibid., pp. 12, 13, 14, 15. Freud's example came from James G. Frazer, *Totemism and Exogamy*, 4 vols. (London, 1910), 2: 385.

19 Freud, *Totem and Taboo*, pp. 14, 16.

20 Ibid., p. 17.

21 Ibid., p. 17.

22 Freud, "Notes upon a Case of Obsessional Neurosis," p. 239 (emphasis in the original).

23 Ibid., pp. 166–167 (emphasis in the original).

24 Ibid., p. 167.

25 Sigmund Freud, *L'Homme aux rats: Journal d'une analyse*. Translated by Elza Ribeiro Hawalka (Paris: Presses Universitaires de France, 1974), p. 46.

26 Freud, "Notes upon a Case of Obsessional Neurosis," pp. 158, 160–162, 178–180 (emphasis in the original).

27 Ibid., p. 182 (emphasis in the original).

28 November 6, 1907, *Minutes of the Vienna Psychoanalytic Society*. Edited by Herman Nunberg and Ernst Federn. Translated by M. Nunberg, 4 vols. (New York: International Universities Press, 1962–1975), 1: 236.

29 Freud, "Notes upon a Case of Obsessional Neurosis," pp. 261, 203–205 (emphasis in the original); see also Freud, *L'Homme aux rats*, pp. 97–103.

30 Freud, "Notes upon a Case of Obsessional Neurosis," pp. 205–206.

31 Ibid., p. 207*n*.

32 Freud, *Totem and Taboo*, p. 36.

33 Ibid., pp. 44–45, 50. Freud's material came from James G. Frazer, *Taboo and the Perils of the Soul* (London, 1911), pp. 3 ff.

34 Freud, *Totem and Taboo*, pp. 54–55, 58, 63.

35 Ibid., pp. 100, 107 (emphasis in the original).

36 Ibid., p. 108.

37 Ibid., p. 125. Freud was quoting Charles Darwin, *The Descent of Man, and Selection in Relation to Sex* (1871), in *The Works of Charles Darwin*. Edited by Paul H. Barrett and R. B. Freeman (London: William Pickering, 1986), 22: 615. Darwin, in turn, was quoting from an article by Dr. Savage in *Boston Journal of Natural History* 5 (1845–1847): 423.

38 Freud, *Totem and Taboo*, p. 141.

39 Ibid., p. 127.

40 Freud, "Analysis of a Phobia in a Five-Year-Old Boy" (1909), *SE* 10: 141, 6, 142, 7, 10, 22.

41 Ibid., pp. 24, 124 (emphasis in the original).

42 Ibid. pp. 7, 9, 13, 14. Strachey translated "Wiwimacher" as "widdler."

43 Ibid., p. 145.

44 Ibid., pp. 40, 41, 122, 123, 37, 39.

45 Ibid., pp. 41–42, 123.

46 Freud, *Totem and Taboo*, p. 129.

47 Ibid., p. 132.

48 Freud to Fliess, September 21, 1897, *The Complete Letters of Sigmund Freud to Wilhelm Fliess*. Translated and edited by Jeffrey Moussaieff Masson (Cambridge, MA: Harvard University Press, 1985), p. 264.

49 See Philip Rieff, *Freud: The Mind of the Moralist*, 3rd edn (Chicago, IL: University of Chicago Press, 1979), p. 187; see also Philip Rieff, "The Meaning of History and Religion in Freud's Thought," in Bruce Mazlish, ed. *Psychoanalysis and History* (Englewood Cliffs, NJ: Prentice-Hall, 1963), pp. 23–44.

50 Freud, "Five Lectures on Psycho-Analysis," pp. 16–17 (emphasis in the original).

51 Freud, *Totem and Taboo*, p. 139. Years later Freud acknowledged that Robertson-Smith's suppositions had lost favor with anthropologists and that "totally divergent theories" had replaced them. He, however, was unmoved. He remained unconvinced "either . . . of Robertson-Smith's errors" or "of the correctness of these innovations." Above all, he added, he was not an anthropologist, but a psychoanalyst and he had a right to take from anthropological literature "what he might need for the work of analysis." Freud, *Moses and Monotheism: Three Essays* (1939), in *SE* 23: 131. See also Edwin R. Wallace, IV, *Freud and Anthropology: A History and Reappraisal*, Psychological Issues, Monograph 55 (New York: International Universities Press, 1983).

52 Freud, *Totem and Taboo*, p. 140.

53 Ibid., pp. 141–142, 143, 146.

54 Ibid., pp. 143, 145 (emphasis in the original).

55 Ibid., p. 158. On the question of transmission, see Robert A. Paul, "Did the Primal Crime Take Place?" *Ethos* 4 (1976): 311–352.

56 Freud, *Totem and Taboo*, pp. 159, 160–161 (emphasis in the original).

57 Freud, "Some Character-Types Met with in Psycho-Analytic Work" (1916), in *SE* 14: 332.

58 Ibid., p. 333.

59 Freud, *Totem and Taboo*, p. 159.

60 Freud, *The Ego and the Id* (1923), in *SE* 19: 52.

61 The Kleinians insisted and still insist on spelling fantasy with a *ph* to differentiate unconscious fantasy from the popular understanding of the word. American authors, however, have tended to stick with the *f.*

62 Richard Wollheim, *The Mind and Its Depths* (Cambridge, MA: Harvard University Press, 1993), p. 155 (emphasis added).

63 Freud to Jung, March 21, 1912, *The Freud/Jung Letters: The Correspondence between Sigmund Freud and C. G. Jung.* Edited by William McGuire. Translated by Ralph Manheim and R. F. C. Hull (Princeton, NJ: Princeton University Press, 1974), p. 495.

64 Freud, "Some Character-Types," p. 333.

65 Freud, *Totem and Taboo,* p. 157.

66 Freud, "Some Character-Types," p. 333.

67 Melanie Klein, "Criminal Tendencies in Normal Children" (1927), in *The Writings of Melanie Klein,* under the general editorship of Roger Money-Kryle, in collaboration with Betty Joseph, Edna O'Shaughnessy, and Hanna Segal (London: Hogarth Press, 1975). Vol. 1, *Love, Guilt and Reparation and Other Works 1921–1945,* p. 182.

2 Reparation gone awry

1 Freud, *Group Psychology and the Analysis of the Ego* (1921), in *SE* 18: 128*n*, 122, 123.

2 Sándor Ferenczi, "Freud's 'Group Psychology and the Analysis of the Ego': Its Contributions to the Psychology of the Individual," in Sándor Ferenczi, *Final Contributions to the Problems and Methods of Psycho-Analysis.* Edited by Michael Balint. Translated by Eric Mosbacher (London: Hogarth Press, 1955; reprint, London: Karnac, Maresfield Reprints, 1980), p. 372. For other assessments, see Ethel Spector Person, ed., *On Freud's "Group Psychology and the Analysis of the Ego"* (Hillsdale, NJ: Analytic Press, 2001).

3 Ernest Jones, *The Life and Work of Sigmund Freud.* Vol. 3, *The Last Phase 1919–1939* (New York: Basic Books, 1957), p. 339.

4 Ferenczi to Freud, April 18, 1920, *The Correspondence of Sigmund Freud and Sándor Ferenczi.* Vol. 3, *1920–1933.* Edited by Ernst Falzeder and Eva Brabant. Translated by Peter T. Hoffer (Cambridge, MA: Harvard University Press, 2000), p. 16 (emphasis in the original).

5 Melanie Klein, "Criminal Tendencies in Normal Children" (1927), in *The Writings of Melanie Klein,* under the general editorship of Roger Money-Kyrle, in collaboration with Betty Joseph, Edna O'Shaughnessy, and Hanna Segal (London: Hogarth Press, 1975). Vol. 1, *Love, Guilt and Reparation and Other Works 1921–1945,* pp. 176, 175.

6 Freud, *Group Psychology,* pp. 73, 75–76.

7 Josef Breuer and Sigmund Freud, *Studies on Hysteria* (1893–1895), in *SE* 2: 108, 109–110.

8 Freud, "Freud's Psycho-Analytic Procedure" (1904), in *SE* 7: 250; see also Freud, *The Interpretation of Dreams* (1900), in *SE* 4: 101.

9 Breuer and Freud, *Studies on Hysteria,* pp. 302–303; see also Freud, *The Interpretation of Dreams,* pp. 531–532.

10 Freud, "Fragment of an Analysis of a Case of Hysteria" (1905), in *SE* 7: 116.

11 Sándor Ferenczi, "Introjection and Transference" (1909), in Sándor Ferenczi, *First Contributions to Psycho-Analysis.* Translated by Ernest Jones (London: Hogarth Press, 1951; reprint, London: Karnac, Maresfield Reprints, 1980), p. 67 (emphasis in the original).

12 Freud, *Group Psychology*, pp. 90–91.
13 Ibid., pp. 91–92.
14 Freud, *Group Psychology*, p. 96.
15 Ibid., p. 94.
16 Ibid., p. 103.
17 Freud, "Fragment of an Analysis," pp. 83, 22.
18 Ibid., pp. 39, 40 (emphasis in the original). Freud explored only cursorily, almost as an afterthought, Dora's homosexual love for Frau K: ibid., pp. 59–63, 110*n*.
19 Freud, *Group Psychology*, p. 108.
20 Freud, "Fragment of an Analysis," p. 82.
21 Freud, *Group Psychology*, pp. 105, 107, 108.
22 Ibid., p. 106.
23 Freud, "Mourning and Melancholia" (1917), in *SE* 14: 249.
24 Freud, *Leonardo da Vinci and a Memory of His Childhood* (1910), in *SE* 11: 100, 102.
25 Ibid., p. 100.
26 December 1, 1909, *Minutes of the Vienna Psychoanalytic Society*. Edited by Herman Nunberg and Ernst Federn. Translated by M. Nunberg, 4 vols. (New York: International Universities Press, 1961–1975), 3: 343.
27 Freud, "On Narcissism: An Introduction" (1914), in *SE* 14: 94. For commentary on Freud's paper, see Joseph Sandler, Ethel Spector Person, and Peter Fonagy, eds., *Freud's "On Narcissism: An Introduction"* (New Haven, CT: Yale University Press, 1991).
28 See Freud, "On Narcissism," p. 100; compare ibid., p. 96.
29 Freud, *Group Psychology*, p. 110.
30 Ibid., pp. 117, 116, 121 (emphasis in the original).
31 Ibid., pp. 124–125, 110 (emphasis in the original).
32 Ibid., pp. 131, 132.
33 See Melanie Klein, "On Identification" (1955), in *The Writings of Melanie Klein*. Vol. 3, *Envy and Gratitude and Other Works 1946–1963* (London: Hogarth Press, 1975) p. 145*n*1.
34 Freud, *Group Psychology*, p. 130.
35 Edward Glover, Scientific Discussion at the Meeting held on October 21, 1942, in Pearl King and Riccardo Steiner, eds., *The Freud-Klein Controversies 1941–45* (London: Routledge, 1991), p. 216.
36 The paper had been circulated prior to the meeting and was taken as read.
37 Paula Heimann, "Some Aspects of the Role of Introjection and Projection in Early Development," in King and Steiner, eds., *The Freud-Klein Controversies*, p. 511.
38 Freud, "Negation" (1925), in *SE* 19: 236–237.
39 Heimann, "Introjection and Projection in Early Development," p. 507.
40 Melanie Klein, "The Origins of Transference" (1952), in *Envy and Gratitude*, p. 49.
41 Freud, *The Ego and the Id* (1923), in *SE* 19: 29.
42 Heimann, "Introjection and Projection in Early Development," pp. 525, 522.
43 Marjorie Brierley, Sixth Discussion of Scientific Controversies, October 20, 1943, in King and Steiner, eds. *The Freud-Klein Controversies*, pp. 538–539.
44 Susan Isaacs, Sixth Discussion of Scientific Controversies, October 20, 1943, in King and Steiner, eds., *The Freud-Klein Controversies*, p. 555 (emphasis in the original).
45 Richard Wollheim, *The Mind and Its Depths* (Cambridge, MA: Harvard University Press, 1993), p. 71.

46 Heimann, "Introjection and Projection in Early Development," p. 524.
47 See Melanie Klein, Joan Riviere, M. N. Searl, Ella F. Sharpe, Edward Glover, and Ernest Jones, "Symposium on Child Analysis," *IJP* 8 (1927): 331–391.
48 *The Writings of Melanie Klein*. Vol. 2, *The Psycho-Analysis of Children*. Translated by Alix Strachey (London: Hogarth Press, 1975), pp. 35–36.
49 Melanie Klein, Manuscript of a lecture about Erna (probably 1924/1925, unpublished), quoted in Claudia Frank and Heinz Weiß, "The Origins of Disquieting Discoveries by Melanie Klein: The Possible Significance of the Case of 'Erna,'" *IJP* 77 (1996): 1107.
50 Klein, *Psycho-Analysis of Children*, pp. 41, 40.
51 Ibid., p. 130.
52 Ibid., pp. 137, 140.
53 Ibid., p. 52.
54 Melanie Klein, "Symposium on Child Analysis" (1927), in *Love, Guilt and Reparation*, p. 161.
55 Klein, *Psycho-Analysis of Children*, p. 52.
56 Joan Riviere, "A Contribution to the Analysis of the Negative Therapeutic Reaction" (1936), in Joan Riviere, *The Inner World and Joan Riviere: Collected Papers 1920–1958*. Edited by Athol Hughes (London: Karnac, 1991), pp. 142, 151.
57 Melanie Klein, "Infantile Anxiety Situations Reflected in a Work of Art and in the Creative Impulse" (1929), in *Love, Guilt and Reparation*, pp. 210–211, 214.
58 Melanie Klein, "On the Theory of Anxiety and Guilt" (1948), in *Envy and Gratitude*, p. 32.
59 Melanie Klein, "The Emotional Life and Ego-Development of the Infant with Special Reference to the Depressive Position," in King and Steiner, eds., *The Freud-Klein Controversies*, p. 756. During the Controversial Discussions, Klein took care not to turn the death instinct into a shibboleth:

> [H]er conclusions [she declared] did not stand or fall on the concept of the death instinct. Many colleagues had come to conclusions similar to hers without believing in the death instinct. She did not think the difference of opinion need affect later conclusions. It is known that aggression is stirred by frustration, and that the first frustration occurs at birth.

Eighth Discussion of the Scientific Differences, February 16, 1944, in ibid., pp. 747–748. See also Meira Likierman, "Primitive Object Love in Melanie Klein's Thinking," *IJP* 74 (1993): 241–253, and Meira Likierman, *Melanie Klein: Her Work in Context* (London: Continuum, 2001).
60 See Melanie Klein, "On Observing the Behaviour of Young Infants" (1952), in *Envy and Gratitude*, p. 96.
61 See Melanie Klein, "A Contribution to the Psychogenesis of Manic-Depressive States" (1935), in *Love, Guilt and Reparation*, p. 275n.
62 Ibid., p. 264.
63 Melanie Klein, Ninth Discussion of Scientific Differences, March 1, 1944, in King and Steiner, eds., *The Freud-Klein Controversies*, p. 799.
64 Klein, "A Contribution to the Psychogenesis of Manic-Depressive States," p. 264.
65 D. W. Winnicott, "The Depressive Position in Normal Emotional Develop-

ment" (1954), in D. W. Winnicott, *Collected Papers: Through Paediatrics to Psycho-Analysis* (London: Tavistock, 1958), p. 265.

66 Klein, "A Contribution to the Psychogenesis of Manic-Depressive States," p. 266.

67 Ibid., p. 270.

68 Klein, "Criminal Tendencies in Normal Children," p. 175.

69 Melanie Klein, "Weaning" (1936), in *Love, Guilt and Reparation*, p. 294.

70 Riviere, "Negative Therapeutic Reaction," pp. 149–150 (emphasis in the original).

71 See Joan Riviere, "The Inner World in Ibsen's *Master-Builder*" (1952), in *The Inner World and Joan Riviere*, pp. 332–347.

72 Ibid., pp. 333, 335–336.

73 Ibid., pp. 337–338.

74 *The Plays of Henrik Ibsen*. Authorized translation (New York: Tudor, 1934), pp. 19, 53–54, 56–58 (emphasis in the original).

75 Ibid. p. 59.

76 Riviere, "Ibsen's *Master-Builder*," p. 338.

77 Riviere, "Negative Therapeutic Reaction," pp. 139, 141 (emphasis in the original).

78 Melanie Klein, "Mourning and its Relation to Manic-Depressive States" (1940), in *Love, Guilt and Reparation*, p. 351 (emphasis in the original).

79 Freud, *Group Psychology*, p. 131.

80 Klein, "Mourning and its Relation to Manic-Depressive States," pp. 362–363.

81 Klein, "On the Theory of Anxiety and Guilt," p. 36.

82 Betty Joseph, "Different Types of Anxiety and their Handling in the Analytic Situation" (1978), in Betty Joseph, *Psychic Equilibrium and Psychic Change: Selected Papers of Betty Joseph*. Edited by Michael Feldman and Elizabeth Bott Spillius (London: Routledge, 1989), p. 107; see also Freud, *Civilization and Its Discontents* (1930), in *SE* 21: 132.

83 Riviere, "Negative Therapeutic Reaction," p. 139.

3 Omnipotence holding sway

1 Freud, *Civilization and Its Discontents* (1930), in *SE* 21: 100–101, 134.

2 Ferenczi to Freud, February 15, 1930, *The Correspondence of Sigmund Freud and Sándor Ferenczi*, vol. 3, *1920–1933*. Edited by Ernst Falzeder and Eva Brabant. Translated by Peter T. Hoffer (Cambridge, MA: Harvard University Press, 2000), p. 389 (emphasis in the original).

3 Joan Riviere, "A Contribution to the Analysis of the Negative Therapeutic Reaction" (1936), in Joan Riviere, *The Inner World and Joan Riviere: Collected Papers 1920–1958*. Edited by Athol Hughes (London: Karnac, 1991), p. 139.

4 Freud, *Civilization and Its Discontents*, pp. 124, 125, 127.

5 Ibid., p. 136.

6 For an attempt to rescue Freud from his inconsistency which rests on the claim that remorse is "an emotion distinct from a sense of guilt," see John Deigh, *The Sources of Moral Agency: Essays in Moral Psychology and Freudian Theory* (Cambridge: Cambridge University Press, 1996), p. 89.

7 Melanie Klein, "Criminal Tendencies in Normal Children" (1927), in *The Writings of Melanie Klein*, under the general editorship of Roger Money-Kyrle, in collaboration with Betty Joseph, Edna O'Shaughnessy, and Hanna Segal (London: Hogarth Press, 1975). Vol. 1, *Love, Guilt and Reparation and Other Works 1921–1945*, pp. 171–172.

8 Melanie Klein, "Symposium on Child Analysis" (1927), in *Love, Guilt and Reparation*, pp. 157–158.

9 Freud, *New Introductory Lectures*, p. 67. When, in *The Ego and the Id*, Freud had initially used the term "super-ego" he had considered it to be synonymous with ego ideal. After close to a decade, during which "ego ideal" failed to reappear in print, he attempted in the *New Introductory Lectures on Psycho-Analysis* (1933) to define it once more.

10 Melanie Klein, "Mourning and its Relation to Manic-Depressive States" (1940), in *Love, Guilt and Reparation*, p. 362.

11 Freud, *Civilization and Its Discontents*, pp. 127–128.

12 Ibid., pp. 130, 12, 128.

13 Ibid., p. 130.

14 Ibid., p. 103n1.

15 Ibid., p. 130.

16 Melanie Klein, "The Early Development of Conscience in the Child" (1933), in *Love, Guilt and Reparation*, p. 251.

17 Paula Heimann and Susan Isaacs, "Regression," in Pearl King and Riccardo Steiner, eds, *The Freud-Klein Controversies 1941–45* (London: Routledge, 1991), p. 697.

18 Freud, *Inhibitions, Symptoms and Anxiety* (1926), in *SE* 20: 115.

19 Melanie Klein, "A Contribution to the Psychogenesis of Manic-Depressive States" (1935), in *Love, Guilt and Reparation*, pp. 273–274.

20 Ibid., p. 274 (emphasis in the original).

21 Melanie Klein, "On the Theory of Anxiety and Guilt" (1948), in *The Writings of Melanie Klein*. Vol. 3, *Envy and Gratitude and Other Works 1946–1963* (London: Hogarth Press, 1975), p. 37 (emphasis in the original).

22 Freud, "Recommendations to Physicians Practicing Psychoanalysis" (1912), in *SE* 12: 113.

23 *The Writings of Melanie Klein*. Vol. 4, *Narrative of a Child Analysis: The Conduct of the Psycho-Analysis of Children as Seen in the Treatment of a Ten-year-old Boy* (London: Hogarth Press, 1975), p. 11.

24 Ibid., pp. 16–17, 13.

25 Ibid., p. 15.

26 *The Writings of Melanie Klein*. Vol. 2, *The Psycho-Analysis of Children*. Translated by Alix Strachey (London: Hogarth Press, 1975), p. 58.

27 Elisabeth R. Geleerd, "Evaluation of *Narrative of a Child Analysis*, by Melanie Klein." *IJP* 44 (1963): 500. See also Hanna Segal and Donald Meltzer, "Evaluation of *Narrative of a Child Analysis*, by Melanie Klein." *IJP* 44 (1963): 507–513.

28 Klein, *Narrative of a Child Analysis*, pp. 19–20, 21–22 (emphasis in the original).

29 Ibid, pp. 127–129 (emphasis in the original).

30 Melanie Klein, "Notes on Some Schizoid Mechanisms" (1946), in *Envy and Gratitude*, p. 1.

31 Freud, "Psycho-Analytic Notes on an Autobiographical Account of a Case of Paranoia (Dementia Paranoides)" (1911), in *SE* 12: 68.

32 Ibid., p. 70.

33 Klein, "Notes on Some Schizoid Mechanisms," p. 23.

34 Freud, *An Outline of Psycho-Analysis* (1940), in *SE* 23: 203.

35 Freud, "Splitting of the Ego in the Process of Defence" (1940), in *SE* 23: 276.

36 Klein, "Notes on Some Schizoid Mechanisms," pp. 6, 10.

37 Ibid., pp. 6, 8, 10 (emphasis in the original).

38 Melanie Klein, "A Note on Depression in the Schizophrenic" (1960), in *Envy and Gratitude*, p. 265. See also Melanie Klein, "Depression: Contribution to the Symposium on Depression" (1959): PP/KLE/C.73, Melanie Klein Archive, Wellcome Library, London.

39 Klein, "A Note on Depression in the Schizophrenic," p. 266. Here Klein drew on Hanna Segal's article, "Depression in the Schizophrenic," *IJP* 37 (1956): 339–343; reprinted in Hanna Segal, *The Work of Hanna Segal* (New York: Jason Aronson, 1981), pp. 121–130.

40 Riviere, "A Contribution to the Analysis of the Negative Therapeutic Reaction," p. 138.

41 John Steiner, *Psychic Retreats: Pathological Organizations in Psychotic, Neurotic and Borderline Patients* (London: Routledge, 1993), p. 89.

42 Hanna Segal, *Psychoanalysis, Literature and War: Papers 1972–1995* (London: Routledge, 1997), p. 62. The article was previously published as "A Delusional System as a Defence Against the Re-emergence of a Catastrophic Situation," *IJP* 53 (1972): 393–401.

43 Freud, "Psycho-Analytic Notes on an Autobiographical Account of a Case of Paranoia," pp. 18, 70.

44 Klein, "Notes on Some Schizoid Mechanisms," p. 23.

45 Segal, *Psychoanalysis, Literature and War*, pp. 49–50.

46 Ibid., pp. 51, 52, 53.

47 Ibid., pp. 55, 56–57.

48 Ibid., pp. 50, 51, 60.

49 Ibid., pp. 61, 52.

50 Ibid., p. 62.

51 John Steiner, "The Retreat from Truth to Omnipotence in Sophocles's *Oedipus at Colonus*," *International Review of Psycho-Analysis* 17 (1990): 227–237; see also John Steiner, "Turning a Blind Eye: The Cover Up for Oedipus," *International Review of Psycho-Analysis* 12 (1985): 161–172. Steiner drew on these two papers for *Psychic Retreats*, ch. 10.

52 Steiner, *Psychic Retreats*, p. 116.

53 Ibid., pp. 120–121.

54 H. I. Pilikian, interview with Douglas Keay, *Guardian*, July 17, 1974, quoted in Steiner, *Psychic Retreats*, pp. 121–122.

55 Philip Vellacott, *Sophocles and Oedipus: A Study of "Oedipus Tyrannus" with a New Translation* (Ann Arbor, MI: University of Michigan Press, 1971), p. 240. Steiner differs with Vellacott on this point. He sees in the self-blinding evidence of guilt turning to hatred and hatred to self-mutilation: *Psychic Retreats*, p. 123.

56 Steiner, *Psychic Retreats*, p. 126.

57 Sophocles, *Oedipus at Colonus*. Translated by Robert Fitzgerald, in *The Complete Greek Tragedies: Sophocles, I*. Edited by David Grene and Richmond Lattimore (Chicago, IL: University of Chicago Press, 1954), pp. 138–140.

58 Freud, *Civilization and Its Discontents*, pp. 112, 129.

4 The ego gaining ground

1 Freud, "Formulations on the Two Principles of Mental Functioning" (1911), in *SE* 12: 222 (emphasis in the original).

2 Freud, *The Ego and the Id* (1923), in *SE* 19: 25.

3 For a helpful discussion of Freud's writings on fantasy, see Joseph Sandler and Humberto Nagara, "Aspects of the Metapsychology of Fantasy," *Psychoanalytic Study of the Child* 18 (1963): 159–194.

4 Hanna Segal, *Dream, Phantasy and Art* (London: Routledge, 1991), p. 19.

5 Betty Joseph, "Psychic Change and the Psychoanalytic Process" (1989), in Betty Joseph, *Psychic Equilibrium and Psychic Change: Selected Papers of Betty Joseph*. Edited by Michael Feldman and Elizabeth Bott Spillius (London: Routledge, 1989), p. 198.

6 See Susan Isaacs, "The Nature and Function of Phantasy," in Pearl King and Riccardo Steiner, eds., *The Freud-Klein Controversies 1941–45* (London: Routledge, 1991). A revised version of Isaacs's paper, with the same title, was subsequently published in *IJP* 29 (1948): 73–97, and Melanie Klein, Paula Heimann, Susan Isaacs, and Joan Riviere, *Developments in Psycho-Analysis*. Edited by Joan Riviere (London: Hogarth Press, 1952), pp. 67–121. For a review of differences between Kleinian and non-Kleinian conceptions of fantasy, see Anne Hayman, "What Do We Mean by 'Phantasy'?" *IJP* 70 (1989): 105–114, and Anne Hayman, "Some Remarks about the 'Controversial Discussions,'" *IJP* 75 (1994): 343–358.

7 Isaacs, "The Nature and Function of Phantasy," pp. 269, 268 (emphasis in the original).

8 Draft of letter from Klein to Jones, ? 1941: PP/KLE/E.6, Melanie Klein Archive, Wellcome Library, London.

> That Freud was not always able to follow up his various findings in all their ramifications is not surprising in view of the enormous and overwhelming wealth of new phenomena with which through his discoveries he was confronted. I will take as an instance the conception of psychic reality, one of F[reud]'s greatest discoveries, and yet one which has not received its full weight in the development of psycho-analysis. This fundamental finding which opened the way to the understanding of phantasy life, has been relatively underrated and neglected; correspondingly the part external reality plays in development and mental life has been overrated, or rather not sufficiently understood in relation to impulses, phantasies, anxieties and guilt. In my work psychic reality and phantasy have received full attention.

9 Isaacs, "The Nature and Function of Phantasy," pp. 276–277 (emphasis in the original).

10 Ernest Jones, First Discussion of Scientific Controversies, January 27, 1943, in King and Steiner, eds., *The Freud-Klein Controversies*, pp. 322–323.

11 Ibid., p. 324.

12 Klein first reported on Erich in "Der Familienromanen in Statu Nascendi," *Internationale Zeitschrift für Psychoanalyse* 6 (1920): 151–155. In this text, never translated and never reprinted, she did not disguise her son's identity. While she was in Slovakia, she decided that in subsequent papers she would give Erich a pseudonym. See Klein to Ferenczi, December 14, 1920, quoted in Phyllis Grosskurth, *Melanie Klein: Her World and Her Work* (New York: Knopf, 1986), p. 91. See also Jean-Michel Petot, *Melanie Klein*. Vol. 1, *First Discoveries and First System 1919–1932*. Translated by Christine Trollope (Madison, CT: International Universities Press, 1990), pp. 14–48.

13 Freud, "Analysis of a Phobia in a Five-Year-Old Boy" (1909), in *SE* 10: 5.

14 Alix to James Strachey, February 11, 1925, *Bloomsbury/Freud: The Letters of James and Alix Strachey 1924–1925* (New York: Basic Books, 1985), p. 201.

15 Melanie Klein, "The Development of a Child" (1921), in *The Writings of Melanie Klein*, under the general editorship of Roger Money-Kyrle, in collaboration

with Betty Joseph, Edna O'Shaughnessy, and Hanna Segal (London: Hogarth Press, 1975). Vol. 1, *Love, Guilt and Reparation and Other Works 1921–1945*, p. 47.

16 In addition to "The Development of a Child," Fritz's treatment was reported on in Melanie Klein, "The Rôle of School in the Libidinal Development of the Child" (1923), in *Love, Guilt and Reparation*, pp. 59–76, and Melanie Klein, "Early Analysis" (1923), in ibid., pp. 77–105.

17 Melanie Klein, "The Psycho-Analytic Play Technique: Its History and Significance" (1955), in *The Writings of Melanie Klein*. Vol. 3, *Envy and Gratitude and Other Works 1946–1963*, p. 123.

18 Klein, "The Development of a Child," pp. 3, 4, 5, 6, 7, 8, 27.

19 See Freud, "Analysis of a Phobia," p. 145.

20 Klein, "The Development of a Child," p. 30.

21 Ibid., pp. 30, 33–34, 40 (emphasis in the original).

22 Klein, "The Rôle of School in the Libidinal Development of the Child," pp. 63, 69–70 (emphasis in the original).

23 Ibid., p. 70n2.

24 Marjorie Brierley, First Discussion of Scientific Controversies," January 27, 1943, in King and Steiner, eds., *The Freud-Klein Controversies*, p. 331.

25 Susan Isaacs, Second Discussion of Scientific Controversies, February 17, 1943, in ibid., p. 368.

26 Klein to Isaacs, May 14, 1943: PP/KLE/E.7, Melanie Klein Archive, Wellcome Library, London.

27 Ibid.

28 Hanna Segal, *Introduction to the Work of Melanie Klein*, enl. edn (London: Hogarth Press, 1978).

29 Ibid., pp. 12, 13, 14, 15.

30 Hanna Segal, *Melanie Klein* (New York: Viking Press, 1980), pp. 136–137.

31 Hanna Segal, "Some Aspects of the Analysis of a Schizophrenic," in Hanna Segal, *The Work of Hanna Segal: A Kleinian Approach to Clinical Practice* (New York: Jason Aronson, 1981), pp. 101–102. This article was originally published in *IJP* 31 (1950): 268–278.

32 Segal, "Some Aspects of the Analysis of a Schizophrenic," pp. 103, 110.

33 Hanna Segal, "Notes on Symbol Formation," in *The Work of Hanna Segal*, pp. 50, 53, 49 (emphasis in the original). This article was originally published in *IJP* 38 (1957): 391–397.

34 Segal, "Notes on Symbol Formation," pp. 54, 53, 55, 57 (emphasis in the original).

35 W. R. Bion, "Differentiation of the Psychotic from the Non-Psychotic Personalities" (1957), in W. R. Bion, *Second Thoughts: Selected Papers in Psycho-Analysis* (London: Heinemann, 1967; reprint, London: Karnac, Maresfield Reprints, 1984), p. 47.

36 W. R. Bion, "On Hallucination" (1958), in *Second Thoughts*, pp. 65–66, 67, 68, 71, 72, 73, 77. For helpful commentary, see Donald Meltzer, *The Kleinian Development: Part III, The Clinical Significance of the Work of Bion* (Perthshire: Clunie Press, 1978).

37 Bion, "Differentiation of the Psychotic from the Non-Psychotic Personalities," pp. 61, 62–63.

38 Melanie Klein, "Notes on Some Schizoid Mechanisms" (1946), in *Envy and Gratitude*, p. 8.

39 W. R. Bion, "Attacks on Linking" (1959), in *Second Thoughts*, p. 103.

40 Ibid., pp. 103–104. According to Hanna Segal, when Klein heard Bion speaking of mothers bearing projective identification, "she threw up her hands and said 'what ever will the mother have to do next.'" But, Segal continued, Klein "didn't interfere with that." See http://www.melanie-klein-trust.org.uk/segalinterview2001.htm, p. 3.

41 Edna O'Shaughnessy, "W. R. Bion's Theory of Thinking and New Techniques in Child Analysis" (1981), in Elizabeth Bott Spillius, ed., *Melanie Klein Today: Developments in Theory and Practice*. Vol. 2, *Mainly Practice* (London: Routledge, 1988), pp. 178, 180. This article was originally published as "A Commemorative Essay on W. R. Bion's Theory of Thinking," *Journal of Child Psychotherapy* 7 (1981): 181–189.

42 Michael Feldman, "Supporting Psychic Change: Betty Joseph," in Edith Hargreaves and Arturo Varchevker, eds., *In Pursuit of Psychic Change: The Betty Joseph Workshop* (Hove, UK: Brunner-Routledge, 2004), p. 22.

43 Freud, *The Ego and the Id* (1923), in *SE* 19: 53.

44 Bion, "Attacks on Linking," p. 107.

45 Betty Joseph, "The Patient Who Is Difficult to Reach" (1975), in *Psychic Equilibrium*, pp. 75, 76.

46 Ibid., pp. 82–84.

47 Betty Joseph, "Psychic Change and the Psychoanalytic Process" (1989), in *Psychic Equilibrium*, pp. 199–200.

48 Betty Joseph, "On Understanding and Not Understanding: Some Technical Issues" (1983), in *Psychic Equilibrium*, p. 148.

49 Joseph, "Psychic Change and the Psychoanalytic Process," p. 198.

50 On the face of it, one cannot simply move from the notion of enlarging the ego to that of diminishing the reach of the superego, that is, posit a smooth progression from the ego's wanting to know to its passing judgment. A substantial bit of philosophical orthodoxy, that is, the fact/value divide, cuts across the path. Or does it? Klein and post-Kleinians, without engaging in abstract speculation, have implicitly taken the line that although a fact/value distinction exists – a modest one – nothing metaphysical follows from it. Indeed, as the philosopher Hilary Putnam persuasively argues, fact and value are deeply entangled and, further, such "entanglement undermines the idea of an omnipresent and all-important gulf between value judgments and . . . statements of fact." Hilary Putnam, *The Collapse of the Fact/Value Dichotomy and Other Essays* (Cambridge, MA: Harvard University Press, 2002), p. 8.

51 Ronald Britton, *Sex, Death, and the Superego: Experiences in Psychoanalysis* (London: Karnac, 2003), p. 10; see also Ronald Britton, "Emancipation from the Super-ego: A Clinical Study of the Book of Job," in David M. Black, ed., *Psychoanalysis and Religion in the 21st Century: Competitors or Collaborators?* (London: Routledge, 2006), pp. 83–96. For a discussion of Strachey's paper, see Judith M. Hughes, *From Obstacle to Ally: The Evolution of Psychoanalytic Practice* (Hove, UK: Brunner-Routledge, 2004), pp. 92–96.

52 Britton, *Sex, Death, and the Superego*, p. 104 (emphasis in the original).

53 Ibid., p. 110.

54 *Job* 1: 8, 11, in *The New Oxford Annotated Bible*, New Revised Standard Version (New York: Oxford University Press, 1991).

55 *Job* 2: 4–8.

56 Jack Miles, *God: A Biography* (New York: Knopf, 1995), p. 314.

57 *Job* 40: 10–14.

58 Miles, *God*, pp. 315, 316 (emphasis in the original).
59 *Job* 40: 4–5.
60 Miles, *God*, p. 317.
61 *Job* 42: 6.
62 Miles, *God*, pp. 323, 324.
63 Britton, *Sex, Death, and the Superego*, pp. 111, 124, 125.
64 Ibid., p. 112. See also Edna O'Shaughnessy, "Relating to the Superego," *IJP* 80 (1999): 861–870.
65 Freud, "Analysis Terminable and Interminable" (1937), in *SE* 23: 235.
66 Isaacs, "The Nature and Function of Phantasy," p. 277.
67 Elizabeth Bott Spillius, "General Introduction," in Spillius, ed., *Melanie Klein Today* 2: 6.
68 Joseph, "The Patient Who Is Difficult to Reach," p. 76.
69 See Feldman, "Supporting Psychic Change," pp. 22, 23, 28.
70 Klein to Isaacs, May 14, 1943.
71 Roy Schafer, "The Contemporary Kleinians of London," *Psychoanalytic Quarterly* 63 (1994): 427.

Conclusion

1 Elsewhere I have recounted the emergence of psychoanalysis as an autonomous discipline: see Judith M. Hughes, *From Freud's Consulting Room: The Unconscious in a Scientific Age* (Cambridge, MA: Harvard University Press, 1994).
2 Draft of letter from Klein to Jones, ? 1941: PP/KLE/E.6, Melanie Klein Archives, Wellcome Library, London.
3 Freud, *The Ego and the Id* (1923), in *SE* 19: 32–33.
4 Freud, *Group Psychology and the Analysis of the Ego* (1921), in *SE* 18: 108, and Freud, "Mourning and Melancholia" (1917), in *SE* 14: 249.
5 Freud, *The Ego and the Id*, p. 34 (emphasis in the original).
6 Freud, *Civilization and Its Discontents* (1930), in *SE* 21: 137.
7 Freud, *Totem and Taboo: Some Points of Agreement between the Mental Lives of Savages and Neurotics* (1913), in *SE* 13: 145 (emphasis in the original).
8 Melanie Klein, "The Origins of Transference" (1952), in *The Writings of Melanie Klein*, under the general editorship of Roger Money-Kyrle, in collaboration with Betty Joseph, Edna O'Shaughnessy, and Hanna Segal (London: Hogarth Press, 1975). Vol. 3, *Envy and Gratitude and Other Works 1946–1963*, p. 49.
9 Melanie Klein, "Mourning and its Relation to Manic-Depressive States" (1940), in *The Writings of Melanie Klein*. Vol. 1, *Love, Guilt and Reparation and Other Works 1921–1945*, p. 362.
10 Freud, *Civilization and Its Discontents*, pp. 124–125.
11 Melanie Klein, "Notes on Some Schizoid Mechanisms" (1946), in *Envy and Gratitude*, p. 1.
12 Joan Riviere, "A Contribution to the Analysis of the Negative Therapeutic Reaction" (1936), in Joan Riviere, *The Inner World and Joan Riviere: Collected Papers 1920–1958*. Edited by Athol Hughes (London: Karnac, 1991), pp. 139–140, 138, 146 (emphasis in the original).
13 Klein, "Notes on Some Schizoid Mechanisms," p. 23.
14 John Steiner, *Psychic Retreats: Pathological Organizations in Psychotic, Neurotic and Borderline Patients* (London: Routledge, 1993), p. 112.
15 James Strachey, "The Nature of the Therapeutic Action of Psycho-Analysis," *IJP* 15 (1934): 133, 137, 138, 146 (emphasis in the original).

16 Betty Joseph, "Psychic Change and the Psychoanalytic Process" (1989), in Betty Joseph, *Psychic Equilibrium and Psychic Change: Selected Papers of Betty Joseph*. Edited by Michael Feldman and Elizabeth Bott Spillius (London: Routledge, 1989), p. 198.

17 Freud, *New Introductory Lectures on Psycho-Analysis* (1933), in *SE* 22: 80.

Selected bibliography

Abraham, Karl. *Selected Papers of Karl Abraham*. Translated by Douglas Bryan and Alix Strachey. London: Hogarth Press, 1927. Reprint, London: Karnac, Maresfield Reprints, 1979.

Aguayo, Joseph. "Patronage and the Dispute over Child Analysis between Melanie Klein and Anna Freud – 1927–1932." *IJP* 81 (2000): 733–752.

—— "Reassessing the Clinical Affinity between Melanie Klein and D.W. Winnicott (1935–51): Klein's Unpublished 'Notes on Baby' in Historical Context." *IJP* 83 (2002): 1133–1152.

Alexander, Franz. "A Metapsychological Description of the Process of Cure." *IJP* 6 (1925): 13–34.

Alfred, Fred C. *Melanie Klein and Critical Social Theory: An Account of Politics, Art and Reason Based on Her Psychoanalytic Theory*. New Haven, CT: Yale University Press, 1989.

Anderson, Robin, ed. *Clinical Lectures on Klein and Bion*. London: Tavistock/Routledge, 1992.

Andreas-Salomé, Lou. *The Freud Journal of Lou Andreas-Salomé*. Translated by Stanley A. Leavy. New York: Basic Books, 1964.

Anzieu, Didier. "Comment devient-on Melanie Klein?" *Nouvelle Revue de Psychanalyse* 26 (1982): 235–251.

Apfelbaum, Bernard. "On Ego Psychology: A Critique of the Structural Approach to Psycho-Analytic Theory." *IJP* 47 (1966): 451–475.

Appignanesi, Lisa, and John Forrester. *Freud's Women*. New York: Basic Books, 1992.

Arlow, Jacob A., and Charles Brenner. *Psychoanalytic Concepts and the Structural Theory*. New York: International Universities Press, 1964.

Bibring, Edward. "The Development and Problems of the Theory of the Instincts." *IJP* 22 (1941): 102–131.

—— "The So-Called English School of Psychoanalysis." *Psychoanalytic Quarterly* 16 (1947): 69–93.

Bion, Francesca, Hanna Segal, Isabel Menzies Lyth, and Donald Meltzer. "Memorial Meeting for Dr. Wilfred Bion." *International Review of Psycho-Analysis* 8 (1981): 3–14.

Bion, Wilfred R. *Experience in Groups and Other Papers*. London: Tavistock, 1961.

—— *Learning from Experience.* London: Heinemann, 1962. Reprint, London: Karnac, Maresfield Reprints, 1984.

—— *Elements of Psycho-Analysis.* London: Heinemann, 1963. Reprint, London: Karnac, Maresfield Reprints, 1984.

—— *Transformations.* London: Heinemann, 1965. Reprint, London: Karnac, Maresfield Reprints, 1984.

—— *Second Thoughts: Selected Papers on Psycho-Analysis.* London: Heinemann, 1967. Reprint, London: Karnac, Maresfield Reprints, 1984.

—— *Attention and Interpretation.* London: Tavistock, 1970. Reprint, London: Karnac, Maresfield Reprints, 1984.

—— *The Long Week-End 1897–1919: Part of a Life.* Edited by Francesca Bion. Abingdon: Fleetwood Press, 1982.

—— *All My Sins Remembered: Another Part of a Life and the Other Side of Genius – Family Letters.* Edited by Francesca Bion. Abingdon: Fleetwood Press, 1985.

—— *Taming Wild Thoughts.* Edited by Francesca Bion. London: Karnac, 1997.

—— *War Memoirs 1917–1919.* Edited by Francesca Bion. London: Karnac, 1997.

Bléandonu, Gérard. *Wilfred Bion: His Life and Works 1897–1979.* Translated by Claire Pajaczkowska. London: Free Association Books, 1994.

Borch-Jacobsen, Mikkel. *The Freudian Subject.* Translated by Catherine Porter. Stanford, CA: Stanford University Press, 1988.

Brenner, Charles. *The Mind in Conflict.* New York: International Universities Press, 1982.

Breuer, Josef, and Sigmund Freud. *Studies on Hysteria* (1895). In *SE*, vol. 2.

Brierley, Marjorie. *Trends in Psycho-Analysis.* London: Hogarth Press, 1951.

Britton, Ronald. "The Blindness of the Seeing Eye: Inverse Symmetry as a Defense Against Reality." *Psychoanalytic Inquiry* 14 (1994): 365–378.

—— *Belief and Imagination: Explorations in Psychoanalysis.* London: Routledge, 1998.

—— *Sex, Death and the Superego: Experiences in Psychoanalysis.* London: Karnac, 2003.

Britton, Ronald, Michael Feldman, and Edna O'Shaughnessy. *The Oedipus Complex Today: Clinical Implications.* London: Karnac, 1989.

Brome, Vincent. *Ernest Jones: Freud's Alter Ego.* New York: Norton, 1983.

Caper, Robert. *Immaterial Facts: Freud's Discovery of Psychic Reality and Klein's Development of His Work.* Northvale, NJ: Jason Aronson, 1988.

—— *A Mind of One's Own: A Kleinian View of Self and Object.* London and New York: Routledge, 1999.

Cavell, Marcia. *The Psychoanalytic Mind: From Freud to Philosophy.* Cambridge, MA: Harvard University Press, 1993.

—— *Becoming a Subject: Reflections in Philosophy and Psychoanalysis.* Oxford: Oxford University Press, 2006.

Compton, Allan. "On the Psychoanalytic Theory of Instinctual Drives. I: The Beginnings of Freud's Drive Theory." *Psychoanalytic Quarterly* 50 (1981): 190–218.

—— "On the Psychoanalytic Theory of Instinctual Drives. II: The Sexual Drives and the Ego Drives." *Psychoanalytic Quarterly* 50 (1981): 219–237.

—— "On the Psychoanalytic Theory of Instinctual Drives. III: The Complications of Libido and Narcissism." *Psychoanalytic Quarterly* 50 (1981): 345–362.

—— "On the Psychoanalytic Theory of Instinctual Drives. IV: Instinctual Drives and the Ego-Id-Superego Model." *Psychoanalytic Quarterly* 50 (1981): 363–392.

Cooper, Arnold M. *The Quiet Revolution in American Psychoanalysis: Selected Papers of Arnold M. Cooper*. Hove, UK: Brunner-Routledge, 2005.

Cottingham, John. *Philosophy and the Good Life: Reason and the Passions in Greek, Cartesian and Psychoanalytic Ethics*. Cambridge: Cambridge University Press, 1998.

Darwin, Charles. *The Works of Charles Darwin*, edited by Paul H. Barrett and R.B. Freeman. Vols. 21–22, *The Descent of Man, and Selection in Relation to Sex* (1871). London: William Pickering, 1986.

Deigh, John. *The Sources of Moral Agency: Essays in Moral Psychology and Freudian Theory*. Cambridge: Cambridge University Press, 1996.

Eissler, Kurt R. "The Effect of the Structure of the Ego on Psychoanalytic Technique." *JAPA* 1 (1953): 104–143.

Ellenberger, Henri. *The Discovery of the Unconscious: The History and Evolution of Dynamic Psychiatry*. New York: Basic Books, 1970.

Etchegoyen, R. Horacio. "Fifty Years after the Mutative Interpretation." *IJP* 64 (1983): 445–459.

—— *The Fundamentals of Psychoanalytic Technique*. Translated by Patricia Pitchon. London: Karnac, 1991.

Fairbairn, W. Ronald D. *Psychoanalytic Studies of the Personality*. London: Tavistock and Routledge and Kegan Paul, 1952.

—— *From Instinct to Self: Selected Papers of W. R. D. Fairbairn*. Vol. 1, *Clinical and Theoretical Papers*. Edited by David E. Scharff and Ellinor Fairbairn Birtles. Vol. 2, *Applications and Early Contributions*. Edited by Ellinor Fairbairn Birtles and David E. Scharff. Northvale, NJ: Jason Aronson, 1994.

Federn, Paul. "Narcissism in the Structure of the Ego." *IJP* 9 (1928): 401–419.

Feldman, Michael. "Common Ground: The Centrality of the Oedipus Complex." *IJP* 71 (1990): 37–48.

—— "Aspects of Reality and the Focus of Interpretation." *Psychoanalytic Inquiry* 13 (1993): 274–295.

—— "The Dynamics of Reassurance." *IJP* 74 (1993): 275–285.

—— "Projective Identification in Phantasy and Enactment." *Psychoanalytic Inquiry* 14 (1994): 423–440.

—— "Projective Identification: The Analyst's Involvement." *IJP* 78 (1997): 227–241.

—— "Some Views on the Manifestation of the Death Instinct in Clinical Work." *IJP* (2000): 53–65.

Ferenczi, Sándor. *First Contributions to Psycho-Analysis*. Translated by Ernest Jones. London: Hogarth Press, 1952. Reprint, London: Karnac, Maresfield Reprints, 1980.

—— *Further Contributions to Psycho-Analysis*, 2nd edn. Edited by John Rickman. Translated by Jane Isabel Suttie. London: Hogarth Press, 1950. Reprint, London: Karnac, Maresfield Reprints, 1980.

—— *Final Contributions to the Problems and Methods of Psycho-Analysis*. Edited by Michael Balint. Translated by Eric Mosbacher. London: Hogarth Press, 1955. Reprint, London: Karnac, Maresfield Reprints, 1980.

—— *The Clinical Diary of Sándor Ferenczi*. Edited by Judith Dupont. Translated by

Michael Balint and Nicola Zarday Jackson. Cambridge, MA: Harvard University Press, 1988.

—— *The Sándor Ferenczi-Georg Groddeck Correspondence 1921–1933*. Edited and annotated by Christopher Fortune. Translated by Jeannie Cohen, Elisabeth Petersdorff, and Norbert Ruebsaat. London: Open Gate Press, 2002.

Ferenczi, Sándor, and Otto Rank. *The Development of Psychoanalysis*. Translated by Caroline Newton. New York: Nervous and Mental Disease Publishing, 1935. Reprint, Madison, CT: International Universities Press, 1986.

Frank, Claudia. "The Discovery of the Child as an Object *Sui Generis* of Cure and Research by Melanie Klein as Reflected in the Notes of Her First Child Analysis in Berlin 1921–1926." *Psychoanalysis and History* 1 (1999): 155–174.

Frank, Claudia, and Heinz Weiß. "The Origins of Disquieting Discoveries by Melanie Klein: The Possible Significance of the Case of 'Erna.'" *IJP* 77 (1996): 1101–1126.

Freud, Anna. *The Writings of Anna Freud*, 8 vols. New York: International Universities Press, 1965–1981.

Freud, Sigmund. *Gesammelte Werke, Chronologisch Geordnet*. Edited by Anna Freud, Edward Bibring, Willi Hoffer, Ernst Kris, and Otto Isakower. Vols. 1–17. London: Imago, 1940–1952. Vol. 18. Frankfurt: S. Fischer, 1968.

—— *The Standard Edition of the Complete Psychological Works of Sigmund Freud*, 24 vols. Translated from the German under the general editorship of James Strachey. London: Hogarth Press, 1953–1974.

—— *Psychoanalysis and Faith: The Letters of Sigmund Freud and Oskar Pfister*. Edited by Heinrich Meng and Ernst L. Freud. Translated by Eric Mosbacher. New York: Basic Books, 1963.

—— *Letters of Sigmund Freud 1873–1939*. Edited by Ernst L. Freud. Translated by Tania Stern and James Stern. London: Hogarth Press, 1970.

—— *The Letters of Sigmund Freud and Arnold Zweig*. Edited by Ernst L. Freud. Translated by Elaine and William Robson-Scott. New York: New York University Press, 1970.

—— *Sigmund Freud and Lou Andreas-Salomé: Letters*. Edited by Ernst Pfeiffer. Translated by Elaine and William Robson-Scott. London: Hogarth Press, 1970.

—— *The Freud/Jung Letters: The Correspondence between Sigmund Freud and C. G. Jung*. Edited by William McGuire. Translated by Ralph Manheim and R. F. C. Hull. Princeton, NJ: Princeton University Press, 1974.

—— *L'Homme aux rats: Journal d'une analyse*. Translated by Elza Riberio Hawalka. Paris: Presses Universitaires de France, 1974.

—— *The Complete Letters of Sigmund Freud to Wilhelm Fliess 1887–1904*. Translated and edited by Jeffrey Moussaiff Masson. Cambridge, MA: Harvard University Press, 1985.

—— *A Phylogenetic Fantasy: An Overview of the Transference Neuroses*. Edited by Ilse Grubrich-Simitis. Translated by Axel Hoffer and Peter T. Hoffer. Cambridge, MA: Harvard University Press, 1987.

—— *The Letters of Sigmund Freud to Eduard Silberstein 1871–1881*. Edited by Walter Boehlich. Translated by Arnold J. Pomerans. Cambridge, MA: Harvard University Press, 1990.

—— *The Diary of Sigmund Freud 1929–1939: A Record of the Final Decade*.

Translated, annotated, with an introduction by Michael Molnar. London: Hogarth Press, 1992.

—— *The Correspondence of Sigmund Freud and Sándor Ferenczi.* Vol. 1, *1908–1914.* Edited by Eva Brabant, Ernst Falzeder, and Patrizia Giampieri-Deutsch. Translated by Peter T. Hoffer. Vol. 2, *1914–1919.* Edited by Ernst Falzeder and Eva Brabant, with the collaboration of Patrizia Giampieri-Deutsch. Translated by Peter T. Hoffer. Vol. 3, *1920–1933.* Edited by Ernst Falzeder and Eva Brabant, with the collaboration of Patrizia Giampieri-Deutsch. Translated by Peter T. Hoffer. Cambridge, MA: Harvard University Press, 1993–2000.

—— *The Complete Correspondence of Sigmund Freud and Ernest Jones 1908–1939.* Edited by R. Andrew Paskauskas. Cambridge, MA: Harvard University Press, 1993.

—— *The Complete Correspondence of Sigmund Freud and Karl Abraham 1907–1925.* Edited by Ernst Falzeder. Translated by Caroline Schwarzacher. London: Karnac, 2002.

—— *The Sigmund-Freud-Ludwig Binswanger Correspondence 1908–1938.* Edited by Gerhard Fichtner. Translated by Arnold J. Pomerans. New York: Other Press, 2003.

Friedman, Lawrence. "The Therapeutic Alliance." *IJP* 50 (1969): 139–153.

—— "Trends in the Psychoanalytic Theory of Treatment." *Psychoanalytic Quarterly* 47 (1978): 524–567.

—— *The Anatomy of Psychotherapy.* Hillsdale, NJ: Analytic Press, 1988.

—— "How and Why Patients Become More Objective? Sterba Compared with Strachey." *Psychoanalytic Quarterly* 61 (1992): 1–17.

—— "Ferrum, Ignis, and Medicina: Return to the Crucible." *JAPA* 45 (1997): 21–36.

Gardiner, Muriel, ed. *The Wolf-Man by the Wolf-Man.* New York: Basic Books, 1971.

Gardiner, Sebastian. *Irrationality and the Philosophy of Psychoanalysis.* Cambridge: Cambridge University Press, 1993.

Gay, Peter. *Freud, Jews, and Other Germans: Masters and Victims in Modernist Culture.* New York: Oxford University Press, 1978.

—— *A Godless Jew: Freud, Atheism, and the Making of Psychoanalysis.* New Haven, CT: Yale University Press, 1987.

—— *Freud: A Life for Our Time.* New York: Norton, 1988.

Gedo, John E., and Arnold Goldberg. *Models of the Mind: A Psychoanalytic Theory.* Chicago, IL: University of Chicago Press, 1973.

Geleerd, Elisabeth R. "Evaluation of *Narrative of a Child Analysis*, by Melanie Klein." *IJP* 44 (1963): 493–506.

Gellner, Ernst. *The Psychoanalytic Movement or The Coming of Unreason.* London: Paladin, 1985.

Gill, Merton M. *Topography and Systems in Psychoanalytic Theory.* Psychological Issues, Monograph 10. New York: International Universities Press, 1963.

Glover, Edward. "The Therapeutic Effect of Inexact Interpretation: A Contribution to the Theory of Suggestion." *IJP* 12 (1931): 397–411.

—— "Review of *The Psychoanalysis of Children*, by Melanie Klein." *IJP* 14 (1933): 119–129.

—— "Examination of the Klein System of Child Psychology." *Psychoanalytic Study of the Child* 1 (1945): 75–118.

—— "The Position of Psycho-Analysis in Britain." *British Medical Bulletin* 6 (1949): 27–31. (Also published in Edward Glover. *On the Early Development of Mind.* London: Imago, 1956.)

—— *The Technique of Psycho-Analysis.* London: Baillière, Tindall and Cox, 1955.

Glover, Edward, Otto Fenichel, James Strachey, Edmund Bergler, Herman Nunberg, and Edward Bibring. "Symposium on the Theory of the Therapeutic Results of Psycho-Analysis." *IJP* 18 (1937): 125–195.

Gray, Paul. *The Ego and the Analysis of Defense.* Northvale, NJ: Jason Aronson, 1994.

Green, André. *On Private Madness.* London: Hogarth Press, 1986.

Greenberg, Jay R., and Stephen A. Mitchell. *Object Relations in Psychoanalytic Theory.* Cambridge, MA: Harvard University Press, 1983.

Grinberg, Léon, Darío Sor, and Elizabeth Tabak de Bianchedi. *New Introduction to the Work of Bion.* Northvale, NJ: Jason Aronson, 1971.

Groddeck, Georg W. *The Book of the It.* Translated by V. M. E. Collins. London: Vision Press, 1949.

Grosskurth, Phyllis. *Melanie Klein: Her World and Her Work.* New York: Knopf, 1986.

Grotstein, James S., ed. *Do I Dare Disturb the Universe? A Memorial to Wilfred R. Bion.* Beverly Hills, CA: Caesura Press, 1981. Reprint, London: Karnac, Maresfield Reprints, 1983.

—— *Splitting and Projective Identification.* New York: Jason Aronson, 1981.

—— "The Significance of Kleinian Contributions to Psychoanalysis I. Kleinian Instinct Theory." *International Journal of Psychoanalytic Psychotherapy* 8 (1980–1981): 375–392.

—— "The Significance of Kleinian Contributions to Psychoanalysis II. Freudian and Kleinian Conceptions of Early Mental Development." *International Journal of Psychoanalytic Psychotherapy* 8 (1980–1981): 393–428.

—— "The Significance of Kleinian Contributions to Psychoanalysis III. The Kleinian Theory of Ego Psychology and Object Relations." *International Journal of Psychoanalytic Psychotherapy* 9 (1982–1983): 487–510.

—— "The Significance of Kleinian Contributions to Psychoanalysis IV. Critiques of Klein." *International Journal of Psychoanalytic Psychotherapy* 9 (1982–1983): 511–535.

Grotstein, James, and Donald B. Rinsley, eds. *Fairbairn and the Origins of Object Relations.* New York: Guilford, 1994.

Grubich-Simitis, Ilse. *Back to Freud's Texts: Making Silent Documents Speak.* New Haven, CT: Yale University Press, 1996.

Guntrip, Harry. *Personality Structure and Human Interaction: The Developing Synthesis of Psychodynamic Theory.* London: Hogarth Press, 1961.

—— *Schizoid Phenomena, Object-Relations and the Self.* London: Hogarth Press, 1968.

—— *Psychoanalytic Theory, Therapy, and the Self.* New York: Basic Books, 1971. Reprint, London: Karnac, Maresfield Reprints, 1977.

Hacking, Ian. *Representing and Intervening: Introductory Topics in the Philosophy of Science.* Cambridge: Cambridge University Press, 1983.

—— *The Social Construction of What?* Cambridge, MA: Harvard University Press, 1999.

Hale, Nathan G. Jr. *Freud in America.* Vol. 1, *Freud and the Americans: The Beginnings of Psychoanalysis in the United States, 1876–1917.* Vol. 2, *The Rise and Crisis of Psychoanalysis in the United States: Freud and the Americans, 1917–1985.* New York: Oxford University Press, 1971–1995.

—— ed. *James Jackson Putnam and Psychoanalysis: Letters between Putnam and Sigmund Freud, Ernest Jones, William James, Sándor Ferenczi, and Morton Prince, 1877–1917.* Cambridge, MA: Harvard University Press, 1971.

Hargreaves, Edith, and Arturo Varchevker, eds. *In Pursuit of Psychic Change: The Betty Joseph Workshop.* Hove, UK: Brunner-Routledge, 2004.

Hartmann, Heinz. *Ego Psychology and the Problem of Adaptation* (1939). Translated by David Rapaport. New York: International Universities Press, 1958.

—— *Essays on Ego Psychology: Selected Problems in Psychoanalytic Theory.* New York: International Universities Press, 1964.

Hayman, Anne. "What Do We Mean by 'Phantasy'?" *IJP* 70 (1989): 105–114.

—— "Some Remarks about the 'Controversial Discussions.'" *IJP* 75 (1994): 343–358.

Heimann, Paula. *About Children and Children No-Longer.* Edited by Margaret Tonnesmann. London and New York: Tavistock/Routledge, 1989.

Hinshelwood, R. D. *A Dictionary of Kleinian Thought.* London: Free Association Books, 1991.

—— *Clinical Klein.* London: Free Association Books, 1994.

—— "The Elusive Concept of 'Internal Objects' (1934–1943): Its Role in the Formation of the Klein Group." *IJP* 78 (1997): 877–897.

—— "Countertransference." *IJP* 80 (1999): 797–818.

Horney, Karen. "The Problem of the Negative Therapeutic Reaction." *Psychoanalytic Quarterly* 5 (1936): 29–45.

Hughes, Athol. "Letters of Sigmund Freud to Joan Riviere (1921–1939)." *International Review of Psycho-Analysis* 19 (1992): 265–284.

—— "Personal Experiences – Professional Interests: Joan Riviere and Femininity." *IJP* 78 (1997): 899–911.

Hughes, H. Stuart. *Consciousness and Society: The Reorientation of European Social Thought 1890–1930*, rev. edn. New York: Vintage, 1977.

Hughes, Judith M. *Reshaping the Psychoanalytic Domain: The Work of Melanie Klein, W. R. D. Fairbairn, and D. W. Winnicott.* Berkeley, CA: University of California Press, 1989.

—— "Psychoanalysis as a General Psychology, Revisited." *Free Associations* 23 (1991): 357–370.

—— *From Freud's Consulting Room: The Unconscious in a Scientific Age.* Cambridge, MA: Harvard University Press, 1994.

—— "Another Impossible Profession?" *Psychohistory Review* 25 (1997): 119–126.

—— *Freudian Analysts/Feminist Issues.* New Haven, CT: Yale University Press, 1999.

—— *From Obstacle to Ally: The Evolution of Psychoanalytic Practice.* Hove, UK: Brunner-Routledge, 2004.

Ibsen, Henrik. *The Plays of Henrik Ibsen.* Authorized translation. New York: Tudor, 1934.

Jacobson, Edith. *The Self and the Object World.* New York: International Universities Press, 1964.

Joffe, Walter. "A Critical Review of the Status of the Envy Concept." *IJP* 50 (1969): 533–545.

Jones, Ernest. "The Origin and Structure of the Super-Ego." *IJP* 7 (1926): 303–311.

——— *Papers on Psycho-Analysis*, 5th edn. London: Ballière, Tindall and Cox, 1948. Reprint. London: Karnac, Maresfield Reprints, 1977.

——— *The Life and Work of Sigmund Freud.* Vol. 1, *The Formative Years and the Great Discoveries 1856–1900.* Vol. 2, *Years of Maturity 1901–1919.* Vol. 3, *The Last Phase 1919–1939.* New York: Basic Books, 1953–1957.

——— *Free Associations: Memories of a Psycho-Analyst.* New York: Basic Books 1959.

Joseph, Betty. "Persecutory Anxiety in a Four-year-old Boy." *IJP* 47 (1966): 184–188.

——— *Psychic Equilibrium and Psychic Change: Selected Papers of Betty Joseph.* Edited by Michael Feldman and Elizabeth Bott Spillius. London: Routledge, 1989.

——— "Psychic Change: Some Perspectives." *IJP* 73 (1992): 237–243.

——— "Agreeableness as Obstacle." *IJP* 81 (2000): 641–649.

Kernberg, Otto F. *Borderline Conditions and Pathological Narcissism.* New York: Jason Aronson, 1975.

——— *Object Relations Theory and Clinical Psychoanalysis.* New York: Jason Aronson, 1976.

——— *Internal World and External Reality: Object Relations Theory Applied.* New York: Jason Aronson, 1980.

——— *Severe Personality Disorders: Psychotherapeutic Strategies.* New Haven, CT: Yale University Press, 1984.

——— *Aggression in Personality Disorders and Perversions.* New Haven, CT: Yale University Press, 1992.

——— "Convergences and Divergences in Contemporary Psychoanalytic Technique." *IJP* 74 (1993): 659–673.

——— *Love Relations: Normality and Pathology.* New Haven, CT: Yale University Press, 1995.

Khan, M., and Masud R. *Privacy of the Self: Papers on Psychoanalytic Theory and Technique.* London: Hogarth Press, 1974.

——— *Alienation in Perversions.* London: Hogarth Press, 1979.

——— *Hidden Selves: Between Theory and Practice in Psychoanalysis.* London: Hogarth Press, 1983.

King, Pearl H. M. "The Contributions of Ernest Jones to the British Psycho-Analytical Society." *IJP* 60 (1979): 280–284.

——— "The Education of a Psycho-Analyst." Scientific Bulletin, British Psycho-Analytical Society (February 1981): 1–20.

——— "Identity Crises: Splits or Compromises – Adaptive or Maladaptive." In *The Identity of the Psychoanalyst.* Edited by Edward D. Joseph and Daniel Widlöcher. International Psycho-Analytical Association Monographs, no. 2. New York: International Universities Press, 1983.

——— "The Life and Work of Melanie Klein in the British Psycho-Analytical Society." *IJP* 64 (1983): 251–260.

King, Pearl H. M., and Riccardo Steiner, eds. *The Freud-Klein Controversies 1941–45*. London: Routledge, 1991.

Klein, Melanie. "Der Familienromanen in Statu Nascendi." *Internationale Zeitschrift für Psychoanalyse* 6 (1920): 151–155.

—— *The Writings of Melanie Klein*. Vol. 1, *Love, Guilt and Reparation and Other Works 1921–1945*. Vol. 2, *The Psycho-Analysis of Children*. Vol. 3, *Envy and Gratitude and Other Works 1946–1963*. Vol. 4, *Narrative of a Child Analysis: The Conduct of the Psycho-Analysis of Children as Seen in the Treatment of a Ten-year-old Boy*, under the general editorship of Roger Money-Kyrle, in collaboration with Betty Joseph, Edna O'Shaughnessy, and Hanna Segal. London: Hogarth Press, 1975.

Klein, Melanie. Melanie Klein Archive, Wellcome Library, London.

Klein, Melanie, Paula Heimann, Susan Isaacs, and Joan Riviere. *Developments in Psycho-Analysis*. London: Hogarth Press, 1952.

Klein, Melanie, Paula Heimann, and R. E. Money-Kyrle, eds. *New Directions in Psycho-Analysis: The Significance of Infant Conflict in the Pattern of Adult Behaviour*. London: Tavistock, 1955. Reprint, London: Karnac, Maresfield Reprints, 1977.

Klein, Melanie, Joan Riviere, M. N. Searl, Ella F. Sharpe, Edward Glover, and Ernest Jones. "Symposium on Child-Analysis." *IJP* 8 (1927): 331–391.

Kohon, Gregorio, ed. *The British School of Psychoanalysis: The Independent Tradition*. London: Free Association Books, 1986.

Korsgaard, Christine M. *The Sources of Normativity*. Cambridge: Cambridge University Press, 1996.

Kravis, Nathan M. "The 'Prehistory' of the Idea of Transference." *International Review of Psycho-Analysis* 19 (1992): 9–22.

Kris, Anton O. "Helping Patients by Analyzing Self-Criticism." *JAPA* 38 (1990): 605–636.

—— "Freud's Treatment of a Narcissistic Patient." *IJP* 75 (1994): 649–664.

Kris, Ernst. *Selected Papers of Ernst Kris*. New Haven, CT: Yale University Press, 1975.

Laplanche, Jean, and J.-B. Pontalis. "Fantasy and the Origins of Sexuality." *IJP* 49 (1968): 1–18.

—— *The Language of Psycho-Analysis*. Translated by Donald Nicholson-Smith. London: Hogarth Press, 1980.

Lear, Jonathan. *Love and Its Place in Nature: A Philosophical Interpretation of Psychoanalysis*. New Haven, CT: Yale University Press, 1990.

—— *Open Minded: Working Out the Logic of the Soul*. Cambridge, MA: Harvard University Press, 1998.

—— "The Idea of a Moral Psychology: The Impact of Psychoanalysis on Philosophy in Britain." *IJP* 84 (2003): 1351–1361.

—— *Therapeutic Action: An Earnest Plea for Irony*. New York: Other Press, 2003.

—— *Freud*. London: Routledge, 2005.

Likierman, Meira. "Primitive Object Love in Melanie Klein's Thinking: Early Theoretical Influences." *IJP* 74 (1993): 421–253.

—— *Melanie Klein: Her Work in Context*. London: Continuum, 2001.

Lindon, John A. "Melanie Klein's Theory and Technique: Her Life and Work." In

Tactics and Techniques in Psychoanalytic Therapy. Edited by Peter L. Giovacchini. New York: Science House, 1972.

Little, Margaret S. *Transference Neurosis and Transference Psychosis: Toward Basic Unity.* New York: Jason Aronson, 1981.

Loewald, Hans. *Papers on Psychoanalysis.* New Haven, CT: Yale University Press, 1980.

Loewenstein, Rudolph M. *Practice and Precept in Psychoanalytic Technique: Selected Papers of Rudolph M. Loewenstein.* New Haven, CT: Yale University Press, 1982.

López-Corvo, Rafael E. *The Dictionary of the Work of W. R. Bion.* London: Karnac, 2003.

Lyth, Oliver. "Wilfred Ruprecht Bion (1897–1979)." *IJP* 61 (1980): 269–273.

McDougall, Joyce. *Plea for a Measure of Abnormality.* New York: International Universities Press, 1978.

—— *Theaters of the Mind: Illusion and Truth on the Psychoanalytic Stage.* New York: Basic Books, 1985.

—— *Theatres of the Body: A Psychoanalytic Approach to Psychosomatic Illness.* London: Free Association Books, 1989.

McGinn, Colin. *Ethics, Evil, and Fiction.* Oxford: Clarendon Press, 1997.

McGuire, Michael T. *Reconstructions in Psychoanalysis.* New York: Appleton, Century, Crofts, 1971.

McIntosh, Donald. "The Ego and the Self in the Thought of Sigmund Freud." *IJP* 67 (1986): 429–449.

MacIntyre, A. C. *The Unconscious: A Conceptual Analysis.* New York: Humanities Press, 1958.

MacKay, Nigel. "Melanie Klein's Metapsychology: Phenomenological and Mechanistic Perspective." *IJP* 62 (1981): 187–198.

Mahler, Margaret, Fred Pine, and Anni Bergman. *The Psychological Birth of the Human Infant: Symbiosis and Individuation.* New York: Basic Books, 1975.

Mahony, Patrick, Carlo Bonomi, and Jan Stenson, eds. *Behind the Scenes: Freud in Correspondence.* Oslo: Scandinavian University Press, 1997.

Marcus, Steven. *Freud and the Culture of Psychoanalysis: Studies in the Transition from Victorian Humanism to Modernity.* New York: Norton, 1984.

Meisel, Perry, and Walter Kendrick, eds. *Bloomsbury/Freud: The Letters of James and Alix Strachey 1924–1925.* New York: Basic Books, 1985.

Meissner, W. W. *The Paranoid Process.* New York: Jason Aronson, 1978.

Meltzer, Donald. *The Psycho-Analytical Process.* Perthshire: Clunie Press, 1967.

—— *Sexual States of Mind.* Perthshire: Clunie Press, 1973.

—— *The Kleinian Development: Part I, Freud's Clinical Development (Method-Data-Therapy). Part II. Richard Week-by-Week. Part III. The Clinical Significance of the Work of Bion.* Perthshire: Clunie Press, 1978.

—— *Dream-Life: A Re-examination of the Psycho-Analytical Theory and Technique.* Perthshire: Clunie Press, 1984.

—— *Studies in Extended Metapsychology: Clinical Applications of Bion's Ideas.* Perthshire: Clunie Press, 1986.

Mendez, Anita M., and Harold J. Fine, with comments by Harry Guntrip, "A Short History of the British School of Object Relations and Ego Psychology." *Bulletin of the Menninger Clinic* 40 (1976): 357–382.

Midgley, Mary. *The Ethical Primate: Humans, Freedom and Morality*. London: Routledge, 1994.

Miles, Jack. *God: A Biography*. New York: Knopf, 1995.

Milner, Marion. *The Suppressed Madness of Sane Men: Forty-Four Years of Exploring Psychoanalysis*. London: Tavistock, 1987.

Minutes of the Vienna Psychoanalytic Society, 4 vols. Edited by Herman Nunberg and Ernst Federn. Translated by M. Nunberg. New York: International Universities Press, 1962–1975.

Mitchell, Stephen A. "The Origin and Nature of the 'Object' in the Theories of Klein and Fairbairn." *Contemporary Psychoanalysis* 17 (1981): 374–398.

—— *Relational Concepts in Psychoanalysis: An Integration*. Cambridge, MA: Harvard University Press, 1988.

Modell, Arnold H. *Object Love and Reality: An Introduction to a Psychoanalytic Theory of Object Relations*. New York: International Universities Press, 1968.

—— "The Ego and the Id: Fifty Years Later." *IJP* 56 (1975): 57–68.

—— *Other Times, Other Realities: Toward a Theory of Psychoanalytic Treatment*. Cambridge, MA: Harvard University Press, 1990.

Money-Kyrle, Roger. *The Collected Papers of Roger Money-Kyrle*. Edited by Donald Meltzer. Perthshire: Clunie Press, 1978.

Morris, Herbert. *On Guilt and Innocence: Essays in Legal Philosophy and Moral Psychology*. Berkeley, CA: University of California Press, 1976.

Nagel, Thomas. *Other Minds: Critical Essays 1969–1994*. New York: Oxford University Press, 1995.

Neu, Jerome, ed. *The Cambridge Companion to Freud*. Cambridge: Cambridge University Press, 1991.

Novey, Samuel. *The Second Look: The Reconstruction of Personal History in Psychiatry and Psychoanalysis*. Baltimore, MD: Johns Hopkins University Press, 1968.

Nunberg, Herman. "The Synthetic Function of the Ego." *IJP* 12 (1931): 123–140.

O'Shaughnessy, Edna. "A Clinical Study of a Defensive Organization." *IJP* 62 (1981): 359–369.

—— "Enclaves and Excursions." *IJP* 73 (1992): 603–611.

—— "Relating to the Superego." *IJP* 80 (1999): 861–870.

Ogden, Thomas H. *Projective Identification and Psychotherapeutic Technique*. New York: Jason Aronson, 1982.

—— *The Matrix of the Mind: Object Relations and the Psychoanalytic Dialogue*. Northvale, NJ: Jason Aronson, 1986.

Olinik, Stanley L. "The Negative Therapeutic Reaction and Problems of Technique." *IJP* 45 (1964): 540–548.

Paul, Robert A. "Did the Primal Crime Take Place?" *Ethos* 4 (1976): 311–352.

Person, Ethel Spector, ed. *On Freud's "Group Psychology and the Analysis of the Ego."* Hillsdale, NJ: Analytic Press, 2001.

Person, Ethel Spector, Aiban Hagelin, and Peter Fonagy, eds. *On Freud's "Observations on Transference Love."* New Haven, CT: Yale University Press, 1993.

Petot, Jean-Michel. *Melanie Klein*. Vol. 1, *First Discoveries and First System 1919–1932*. Vol. 2, *The Ego and the Good Object 1932–1960*. Translated by Christine Trollope. Madison, CT: International Universities Press, 1990–1991.

Piers, Gerhart, and Milton S. Singer. *Shame and Guilt: A Psychoanalytic and Cultural Study*. New York: Norton, 1971.

Pulver, Sydney E. "Narcissism: The Term and the Concept." *JAPA* 18 (1970): 319–340.

Putnam, Hilary. *The Collapse of the Fact/Value Dichotomy and Other Essays*. Cambridge, MA: Harvard University Press, 2002.

Racker, H. *Transference and Countertransference*. London: Hogarth Press, 1968. Reprint, London: Karnac, Maresfield Library, 1985.

Rapaport, David. *The Structure of Psychoanalytic Theory*. Psychological Issues, Monograph 6. New York: International Universities Press, 1960.

Rawn, Moss L. "Classics Revisited: Some Thoughts on Strachey's 'The Nature of the Therapeutic Action of Psycho-Analysis.'" *IJP* 69 (1988): 507–520.

Richards, Robert J. *Darwin and the Emergence of Evolutionary Theories of Mind and Behavior*. Chicago, IL: University of Chicago Press, 1987.

Rickman, John. *Selected Contributions to Psycho-Analysis*. Edited by W. Clifford M. Scott. London: Hogarth Press, 1957.

Ricoeur, Paul. *Freud and Philosophy: An Essay on Interpretation*. Translated by Denis Savage. New Haven, CT: Yale University Press, 1970.

Rieff, Philip. "The Meaning of History and Religion in Freud's Thought." In *Psychoanalysis and Religion*. Edited by Bruce Mazlish. Englewood Cliffs, NJ: Prentice-Hall, 1963.

—— *Freud: The Mind of the Moralist*. 3rd edn. Chicago, IL: University of Chicago Press, 1979.

Riesenberg-Malcolm, Ruth. *On Bearing Unbearable States of Mind*. London: Routledge, 1999.

Rinsley, Donald B. "Object Relations Theory and Psychotherapy with Particular Reference to the Self-Disordered Patient." In *Technical Factors in the Treatment of the Severely Disturbed Patient*. Edited by Peter L. Giovacchini and L. Bryce Boyer. New York: Jason Aronson, 1982.

Riviere, Joan. *The Inner World and Joan Riviere: Collected Papers 1920–1958*. Edited by Athol Hughes. London: Karnac, 1991.

Roazen, Paul. *Freud and His Followers*. New York: Knopf, 1975.

Robbins, Michael. "Current Controversy in Object Relations Theory as Outgrowth of Schism Between Klein and Fairbairn." *IJP* 61 (1980): 477–492.

Robinson, Paul. *Freud and His Critics*. Berkeley, CA: University of California Press, 1993.

Rosenfeld, Herbert A. "Contributions to the Discussion on Variations in Classical Technique." *IJP* 39 (1958): 238–239.

—— "Discussion on Ego Distortion." *IJP* 39 (1958): 274–275.

—— "An Investigation into the Psycho-Analytic Theory of Depression." *IJP* 40 (1959): 105–129.

—— *Psychotic States: A Psychoanalytical Approach*. London: Hogarth Press, 1965. Reprint, London: Karnac, Maresfield Reprints, 1982.

—— "On the Treatment of Psychotic States by Psychoanalysis: An Historical Approach." *IJP* 50 (1969): 615–631.

—— "A Clinical Approach to the Psychoanalytic Theory of the Life and Death Instincts: An Investigation into the Aggressive Aspects of Narcissism." *IJP* 52 (1971): 169–178.

—— "A Critical Appreciation of James Strachey's Paper on the Nature of the Therapeutic Action of Psychoanalysis." *IJP* 53 (1972): 455–461.

—— "A Discussion of the Paper by Ralph R. Greenson on 'Transference: Freud or Klein.'" *IJP* 55 (1974): 49–51.

—— "Negative Therapeutic Reaction." In *Tactics and Techniques in Psychoanalytic Therapy.* Vol. 2, *Countertransference.* Edited by Peter L. Giovacchini. New York: Jason Aronson, 1975.

—— "Notes on the Psychopathology and Psychoanalytic Treatment of Some Borderline Patients." *IJP* 59 (1978): 215–221.

—— "Some Therapeutic Factors in Psychoanalysis." *International Journal of Psycho-Analysis and Psycho-Therapy* 7 (1978): 152–164.

—— "Primitive Object Relations and Mechanisms." *IJP* 64 (1983): 261–267.

—— *Impasse and Interpretation: Therapeutic and Anti-Therapeutic Factors in the Psychoanalytic Treatment of Psychotic, Borderline, and Neurotic Patients.* London: Tavistock, 1987.

—— *Herbert Rosenfeld at Work: The Italian Seminars.* Edited by Franco De Masi. London: Karnac, 2001.

Rothstein, Arnold. *The Structural Hypothesis: An Evolutionary Perspective.* New York: International Universities Press, 1983.

Rubens, Richard L. "The Meaning of Structure in Fairbairn." *International Review of Psycho-Analysis* 11 (1984): 429–440.

Rudnytsky, Peter L. *Freud and Oedipus.* New York: Columbia University Press, 1987.

Sandler, Joseph. "On the Concept of the Superego." *Psychoanalytic Study of the Child* 15 (1960): 128–162.

—— "Countertransference and Role Responsiveness." *International Review of Psycho-Analysis* 3 (1976): 43–47.

—— "Unconscious Wishes and Human Relationships." *Contemporary Psycho-analysis* 17 (1981): 180–196.

—— "Reflections on Some Relations Between Psychoanalytic Concepts and Psychoanalytic Practice." *IJP* 64 (1983): 35–45.

Sandler, Joseph, with Anna Freud. *The Analysis of Defense: "The Ego and the Mechanisms of Defense" Revisited.* New York: International Universities Press, 1985.

Sandler, Joseph, ed. *Projection, Identification, Projective Identification.* Madison, CT: International Universities Press, 1987.

Sandler, Joseph, and Christopher Dare. "The Psychoanalytic Concept of Orality." *Journal of Psychosomatic Research* 14 (1970): 211–222.

Sandler, Joseph, Christopher Dare, and Alex Holder. *The Patient and the Analyst: The Basis of the Psychoanalytic Process.* London: George Allen and Unwin. 1973.

Sandler, Joseph, and Anna Ursula Dreher. *What Do Psychoanalysts Want? The Problem of Aims in Psychoanalytic Therapy.* London: Routledge, 1996.

Sandler, Joseph, Alex Holder, and Dale Meers. "The Ego Ideal and the Ideal Self." *Psychoanalytic Study of the Child* 18 (1963): 139–158.

Sandler, Joseph, Hansi Kennedy, and Robert L. Tyson. *The Technique of Child Analysis: Discussions with Anna Freud.* Cambridge, MA: Harvard University Press, 1980.

Sandler, Joseph, and Humberto Nagera. "Aspects of the Metapsychology of Fantasy." *Psychoanalytic Study of the Child* 18 (1963): 159–194.

Sandler, Joseph, and Bernard Rosenblatt. "The Concept of the Representational World." *Psychoanalytic Study of the Child* 17 (1962): 128–145.

Sandler, Joseph, and Anne-Marie Sandler. "On the Development of Object Relationships and Affects." *IJP* 59 (1978): 285–296.

—— "The 'Second-Censorship', the 'Three Box Model' and Some Technical Implications." *IJP* 64 (1983): 413–424.

—— "The Past Unconscious, the Present Unconscious, and Interpretation of the Transference." *Psychoanalytic Inquiry* 4 (1984): 367–399.

Sandler, Joseph, Ethel Spector Person, and Peter Fonagy, eds. *Freud's "On Narcissism: An Introduction."* New Haven, CT: Yale University Press, 1991.

Sayers, Janet. *Mothers of Psychoanalysis: Helene Deutsch, Karen Horney, Anna Freud, Melanie Klein.* New York: Norton, 1991.

—— *Kleinians: Psychoanalysis Inside and Out.* Oxford: Polity Press, 2000.

Schafer, Roy. "The Loving and Beloved Superego in Freud's Structural Theory." *Psychoanalytic Study of the Child* 15 (1960): 163–188.

—— *Aspects of Internalization.* New York: International Universities Press, 1968.

—— "The Mechanisms of Defence." *IJP* (1968): 49–62.

—— *A New Language for Psychoanalysis.* New Haven, CT: Yale University Press, 1976.

—— *The Analytic Attitude.* New York: Basic Books, 1983.

—— *Retelling a Life.* New York: Basic Books, 1992.

—— "The Contemporary Kleinians of London." *Psychoanalytic Quarterly* 63 (1994): 409–432.

—— ed. *Contemporary Kleinians of London.* Madison, CT: International Universities Press, 1997.

—— *Bad Feelings.* New York: Other Press, 2003.

—— *Insight and Interpretation: The Essential Tools of Psychoanalysis.* New York: Other Press, 2003.

Scheffler, Samuel. *Human Morality.* New York: Oxford University Press, 1992.

Schmideberg, Melitta. "A Contribution to the History of the Psycho-Analytic Movement in Britain." *British Journal of Psychiatry* 118 (1971): 61–68.

Schreber, Daniel Paul. *Memoirs of My Nervous Illness.* Edited and translated by Ida Macalpine and Richard A. Hunter. Cambridge, MA: Harvard University Press, 1988.

Schur, Max. *Freud: Living and Dying.* New York: International Universities Press, 1972.

Searles, Harold F. *Collected Papers on Schizophrenia and Related Subjects.* New York: International Universities Press, 1965.

—— *Countertransference and Related Subjects: Selected Papers.* New York: International Universities Press, 1979.

—— *My Work with Borderline Patients.* Northvale, NJ: Jason Aronson, 1986.

Segal, Hanna. *Introduction to the Work of Melanie Klein,* enl. edn. London: Hogarth Press, 1978.

—— *Melanie Klein.* New York: Viking Press, 1980.

—— *The Work of Hanna Segal: A Kleinian Approach to Clinical Practice.* New York: Jason Aronson, 1981.

—— *Dream, Phantasy and Art*. London: Routledge, 1991.

—— *Psychoanalysis, Literature and War: Papers 1972–1995*. Edited by John Steiner. London: Routledge, 1997.

—— Interview. http://www.melanie-klein-trust.org.uk/segalinterview2001.htm.

Segal, Hanna, and Donald Meltzer. "Evaluation of *Narrative of a Child Analysis*, by Melanie Klein." *IJP* 44 (1963): 507–513.

Sharpe, Ella Freeman. *Dream Analysis: A Practical Handbook for Psycho-Analysts*. London: Hogarth Press, 1937.

—— *Collected Papers on Psycho-Analysis*. London: Hogarth Press, 1950.

Smith, David L. "Freud's Developmental Approach to Narcissism: A Concise Review." *IJP* 66 (1985): 489–497.

Sophocles. *Oedipus at Colonus*. Translated by Robert Fitzgerald. In *Complete Greek Tragedies: Sophocles, I*. Edited by David Grene and Richmond Lattimore. Chicago, IL: University of Chicago Press, 1954.

—— *Oedipus the King*. Translated by David Grene. In *Complete Greek Tragedies: Sophocles, I*. Edited by David Grene and Richmond Lattimore. Chicago, IL: University of Chicago Press, 1954.

Spillius, Elizabeth Bott. "Some Developments from the Work of Melanie Klein." *IJP* 64 (1983): 321–332.

—— ed. *Melanie Klein Today: Developments in Theory and Practice*. Vol. 1, *Mainly Theory*. Vol. 2, *Mainly Practice*. London: Routledge, 1988.

—— "Developments in Kleinian Thought: Overview and Personal View." *Psychoanalytic Inquiry* 14 (1994): 324–364.

Steiner, John. "The Border between the Paranoid-Schizoid and the Depressive Positions in the Borderline Patient." *British Journal of Medical Psychology* 52 (1979): 385–391.

—— "Perverse Relationships Between Parts of the Self: A Clinical Illustration." *IJP* 63 (1982): 241–252.

—— "Some Reflections on the Analysis of Transference: A Kleinian View." *Psychoanalytic Inquiry* 4 (1984): 443–463.

—— "Turning a Blind Eye: The Cover Up for Oedipus." *International Review of Psycho-Analysis* 12 (1985): 161–172.

—— "Interplay between Pathological Organizations and the Paranoid-Schizoid and Depressive Positions." *IJP* 68 (1987): 69–80.

—— "The Aims of Psychoanalysis." *Psychoanalytic Psychotherapy* 4 (1989): 109–120.

—— "The Psychoanalytic Contribution of Herbert Rosenfeld." *IJP* 70 (1989): 611–617.

—— "Pathological Organizations as Obstacles to Mourning: The Role of Unbearable Guilt." *IJP* 71 (1990): 87–94.

—— "The Retreat from Truth to Omnipotence in Sophocles's *Oedipus at Colonus*." *International Review of Psycho-Analysis* 17 (1990): 227–237.

—— *Psychic Retreats: Pathological Organizations in Psychotic, Neurotic and Borderline Patients*. London: Routledge, 1993.

—— "The Struggle for Dominance in the Oedipus Situation." *Canadian Journal of Psychoanalysis* 7 (1999): 161–177.

Steiner, Riccardo. "Some Thoughts about Tradition and Change Arising from an

Examination of the British Psychoanalytical Society's Controversial Discussions (1943–1944)." *International Review of Psycho-Analysis* 12 (1985): 27–71.

Sterba, Richard. "The Fate of the Ego in Analytic Therapy." *IJP* 15 (1934): 117–126.

—— *Reminiscences of a Viennese Psychoanalyst*. Detroit, MI: Wayne State University Press, 1982.

Stewart, Harold. *Psychic Equilibrium and Problems of Technique*. London: Tavistock/Routledge, 1992.

Stocking, George W. Jr. *After Tylor: British Social Anthropology 1888–1951* Madison, WI: University of Wisconsin Press, 1995.

Strachey, Alix. "A Note on the Use of the Word 'Internal,'" *IJP* 22 (1941): 37–43.

Strachey, James. "The Nature of the Therapeutic Action of Psycho-Analysis." *IJP* 15 (1934): 127–159.

—— "Opening Remarks at a Practical Seminary" (1941). Scientific Bulletin, British Psycho-Analytical Society, July 1988, pp. 15–24. Mimeo.

Sutherland, John D. "Object-Relations Theory and the Conceptual Model of Psychoanalysis." *British Journal of Medical Psychology* 36 (1963): 109–124.

—— *Fairbairn's Journey into the Interior*. London: Free Associations Books, 1989.

Symington, Joan and Neville Symington. *The Clinical Thinking of Wilfred Bion*. London: Routledge, 1996.

Thorner, Hans A. "Notes on the Desire for Knowledge." *IJP* 62 (1981): 73–80.

Tuckett, David. "A Brief View of Herbert Rosenfeld's Contribution to the Theory of Psychoanalytical Technique." *IJP* 70 (1989): 619–625.

Vellacott, Philip. *Sophocles and Oedipus: A Study of "Oedipus Tyrannus" with a New Translation*. Ann Arbor, MI: University of Michigan Press, 1971.

Velleman, J. David. "Love as a Moral Emotion." *Ethics* 109 (1999): 338–374.

—— "A Rational Superego." *Philosophical Review* 108 (1999): 529–558.

—— "The Voice of Conscience." *Proceedings of the Aristotelian Society* 99 (1999): 57–76.

Waelder, Robert. "The Principle of Multiple Function: Observations on Over-Determination." *Psychoanalytic Quarterly* 5 (1936): 45–62.

—— "The Problem of the Genesis of Psychical Conflict in Earliest Infancy: Remarks on a Paper by Joan Riviere." *IJP* 18 (1937): 406–473.

—— "Robert Waelder on Psychoanalytic Technique: Five Lectures." Edited by Samuel A. Guttmann. *Psychoanalytic Quarterly* 56 (1987): 1–67.

Wallace, Edwin R. IV. *Freud and Anthropology: A History and Reappraisal*. Psychological Issues, Monograph 55. New York: International Universities Press, 1983.

Wallerstein, Robert S. "Defenses, Defense Mechanisms, and the Structure of the Mind." *JAPA* (Suppl.) (1983): 201–226.

—— *The Talking Cures: The Psychoanalyses and the Psychotherapies*. New Haven, CT: Yale University Press, 1995.

Weininger, O. *The Clinical Psychology of Melanie Klein*. Springfield, IL: Charles C. Thomas, 1984.

Williams, Bernard. *Ethics and the Limits of Philosophy*. Cambridge, MA: Harvard University Press, 1985.

Winnicott, D. W. *The Maturational Processes and the Facilitating Environment: Studies in the Theory of Emotional Development*. London: Hogarth Press, 1965.

—— *Collected Papers: Through Paediatrics to Psycho-Analysis*. London: Tavistock, 1958.

Wisdom, J. O. "Fairbairn's Contribution on Object Relationship, Splitting, and Ego Structure." *British Journal of Medical Psychology* 36 (1963): 145–159.

—— "Freud and Melanie Klein: Psychology, Ontology, and Weltanschauung." In *Psychoanalysis and Philosophy*. Edited by Charles Hanley and Morris Lazerowitz. New York: International Universities Press, 1970.

Wollheim, Richard. *Sigmund Freud*. New York: Viking Press, 1971. Reprint, Cambridge: Cambridge University Press, 1990.

—— "The Mind and the Mind's Image of Itself," in R. Wollheim, *On Art and the Mind: Essays and Lectures*. London: Allen Lane, 1973.

—— ed. *Freud: A Collection of Critical Essays*. Garden City, NY: Doubleday, 1974.

—— *The Thread of Life*. Cambridge, MA: Harvard University Press, 1984.

—— *The Mind and Its Depths*. Cambridge, MA: Harvard University Press, 1993.

—— *On the Emotions*. New Haven, CT: Yale University Press, 1999.

Wollheim, Richard, and James Hopkins, eds. *Philosophical Essays on Freud*. Cambridge: Cambridge University Press, 1982.

Yorke, Clifford. "Some Suggestions for a Critique of Kleinian Psychology." *Psychoanalytic Study of the Child* 26 (1971): 129–155.

Young, Robert M. *Mental Space*. London: Process Press, 1994.

Index